D1603183

Dooplé

Choreography and Dance Studies

A series of books edited by Robert P. Cohan, C.B.E.

This book is part of a series. The publisher will accept continuation orders which may be cancelled at any time and which provide for automatic billing and shipping of each title in the series upon publication. Please write for details.

Dooplé

The Eternal Law of African Dance

Alphonse Tiérou

Translated from the French by Deirdre McMahon

harwood academic publishers

Switzerland • Australia • Belgium • France • Germany • Gt. Britain •
India • Japan • Malaysia • Netherlands • Russia • Singapore • USA

Harwood Academic Publishers

Private Bag 8
Camberwell, Victoria 3124
Australia

3-14-9, Okubo
Shinjuku, Tokyo 169
Japan

58, rue Lhomond
75005 Paris
France

Emmaplein 5
1075 AW Amsterdam
Netherlands

Glinkastrasse 13-15
0-1086 Berlin
Germany

5301 Tacony Street, Drawer 330
Philadelphia, Pennsylvania 19137
United States of America

Post Office Box 90
Reading, Berkshire RG1 8JL
Great Britain

Originally published in French in 1989 as *DOOPLÉ, LOI ÉTERNELLE DE LA DANSE AFRICAINE* by G.P. Maisonneuve et Larose S.A., Paris.
© 1989 by G.P. Maisonneuve et Larose S.A., Paris.

Cover Photo: A young girl dancing in dooplé: her feet are apart and parallel, her knees are bent, her eyes fixed on the horizon. This characteristic position of traditional African dance was already a feature of early African rock paintings. The body and the face are painted with kaolin which was a symbol of contentment and joy in Africa.

Massango statue, Gabon, in coloured wood. Height 52cm. Marc Felix Collection.

Library of Congress Cataloging-in-Publication Data

Tiérou, Alphonse.
    Dooplé : the eternal law of African dance / Alphonse Tiérou ;
translated from the French by Deirdre McMahon.
      p.   cm. -- (Choreography and dance studies ; v. 2)
    Translation of: Dooplé.
    ISBN 3-7186-5306-0
    1. Dancing--Africa. Sub-Saharan. I. Title. II. Series.
GV1713.S84T545 1992
793.3'1967--dc20
                                        92-19972
                                            CIP

Contents

Introduction to the Series

Choreography and Dance Studies is a book series of special interest to dancers, dance teachers and choreographers. Focusing on dance composition, its techniques and training, the series will also cover the relationship of choreography to other components of dance performance such as music, lighting and training of dancers.

In addition, *Choreography and Dance Studies* will seek to publish new works and provide translations of works not previously published in English, as well as publish reprints of currently unavailable books of outstanding value to the dance community.

Foreword

Few people in the West know much about traditional African dance or are aware that it possesses precise rules and codified movements.

Traditional African dance is an essential element of Africa's cultural heritage because it is the living expression of its philosophy, and the living memory of its evolution and cultural wealth over the centuries.

The African dancer aims at a high level of technique, while maintaining a great respect for the human body.

The richness and wisdom of this dance have been preserved by the society of the Masques de Sagesse (Masks of Wisdom) and those whom they have taught, the "knowing ones". It can still teach us something today.

But western civilisation, as witnessed by the new buildings of Africa, has spread and the number of "knowing ones" has diminished rapidly. Young Africans will soon have only sporadic contact with village life and with the oral culture of the old people.

Moreover West Africa, which has been francophone for generations, has been penetrated by Western culture. Profiting from their innate talents, the children have become accomplished in the European manner. They are writers, lawyers, politicians but have little respect for the originality of their own African culture.

We come from the western part of the Ivory Coast, a mountainous region which was the last to be reached by French civilisation since the Masques de Sagesse had for a long time refused permission for westerners to visit there. We were taught by the Masques of this region, where the traditional culture is still very vibrant, and are members of their society.

We wanted both to protect and make known this cultural heritage to our own world, that of dance. Dance helps to define and explain those rules which constitute a common denominator in all African dances.

The terms used in this book are those of the sacred language of the Grands Masques de l'Ouest (the Grand Masks of the West). Some of the terms have been chosen in order to define precise positions which are not mentioned in the sacred language.

The Ouelou language has not been chosen arbitrarily for the purpose of definition, nor to favour one region more than another, but because this is the language of the Masques de Sagesse de l'Ouest (Masks of Wisdom of the West),[1] and because this is the region which contains some of the most important cultural and artistic discoveries.

Naturally these terms are different in other regions but the choice had to be made.

In writing this book, the first theoretical work about traditional African dance, we wanted to help young Africans to preserve their heritage, to become better acquainted with it and to be proud of it. Living in France and being aware of how ignorant western people are of traditional African dance, we wanted this book to reveal the profound knowledge which it conveys, its ethics and its social role, so that they may better understand the criteria used by Africans and thus be better able to appreciate the performances which they see.

We also wished to facilitate the researches of those who teach African dance, helping them to find within a single volume certain basic elements taught by the Masques, the masters of the dance.

---

1 The closing days (Thursday and Friday) of the International Conference on African Dance, which was held at Yamoussoko from 9 to 15 October 1988, took place at Daloa Man and Dompleu, in western Ivory Coast.

Introduction

Dance is one of those rare human activities which simultaneously reconciles heart, body and spirit.

Dance has existed since the beginning of time and images of dance have been found in the earliest rock paintings. It may have been the first universal form of expression to interpret and communicate the activities and aspirations of man.

The early paintings show various dance forms: the round, the farandole, the open circle, forms which have lasted until today and which testify to the perennial nature of dance in human life.

Although some rock paintings show men assuming the attitudes of hunted animals—with the implication that dance was primarily imitative—others provide evidence that prehistoric man soon had other preoccupations and that he sought to influence the immediate future through dance. Thus it acquired not just an imitative but a "magical" meaning also.

Dance celebrated the worship of divinities. In the West, the religious dances of ancient Greece had an important social role; for example the cult of Athena was the occasion for great festivals.

The Greek texts which have come down to us praised dance both on the physical and the moral level. The ancient Greeks believed that dancing instructed and elevated people while also entertaining them; it was educational and relaxing.[1] In Greece everybody danced; every aspect of life had a place for dance, whether they were private events or local festivities. The dance teaching was very specialised and depended on the standard of the pupils and the type of dances (religious or profane) which were taught.

The early dances can be grouped into two major categories: fertility dances, the fertility of the nourishing earth (sowing, flowering, harvest) but also woman's fertility. These ceremonial dances marked out human life and celebrated the various phases of man's life (birth, initiation, marriage, death). Whatever the motivation of the dance, it combined the spontaneous expression of human feeling with the higher aspirations of man to communicate with the cosmos.

During the Roman empire sacred and profane dances were part of everyday life, urban or peasant. At the end of the empire, Christianity, then just beginning,

---

1 This double role of dance existed in Mesopotamia and Egypt.

1

naturally associated the arts with decadence. From St Paul onwards, the Church distorted the basic meaning of dance, seeing in it only a cult of the body and representing it as the symbol of evil and sin. It wanted to separate what was in fact indivisible: the soul and the body.

In relegating dance to the level of entertainment, the Church was denying both its educational value and its spiritual aspirations.

In the Christian world anything which ennobled and beautified the body, exalted and refined it, or helped to relax it, became "taboo" and was sharply criticised. There were numerous prohibitions on dance. The earliest was that of the Council of Vannes in 465 AD[2] and this was followed by many others. In 1444 the Sorbonne prohibited "the dancing of caroles in the churches during the celebration of divine service", a prohibition repeated by the Council of Trent in 1562 during its great reform of the Church.

Although the Church excommunicated dancers, it was unable to suppress dance completely as an integral part of human nature. It survived throughout the Middle Ages in collective dances: festive peasant dances and aristocratic divertissements in which the search for an aesthetic could be discerned. Both preserved the primitive forms of the round, farandoles or open circles. Gradually the peasant dances became folkloric and were a source of inspiration for other dances in society. The aristocratic dances were codified and preceded the ballets.

Only the dances of death survived in the religious art of the period and they disappeared with the Renaissance.

From the time of Louis XIV onwards the history of western dance, at least in France, has been confused with that of classical dance. The aristocratic dances of the Middle Ages were adapted to the aristocratic life; the steps and the rhythm reflected the way of life of the population which had become middle-class and which had established itself in cities far from the demands of the land and the country way of life. Gradually the ballets of the chateau and the salon gave birth to classical dance.

Classical Dance

It was Charles-Louis Pierre de Beauchamp who first set the five positions of the legs and arms.

> "Beauchamp's principles of action were the same as those of all the official artists of the time, in every discipline. Like Boileau in literature, Le Brun in the arts, Beauchamp wanted to impose universally recognised rules on dance. As with all the arts in the time of Louis XIV, his system emphasised beauty of form and conformity with a fixed canon. This led to a certain rigidity".[3]

2 In 774 Pope Zachary protested in a decree about "the indecent movements of the dance or carole"; in 847 a homily of Pope Leo V condemned "the songs and caroles of women in the Church".
   In 1209 the Council of Avignon decreed that "during the saints' vigils no performances of dance or caroles are to be given".

3 Paul Bourcier, *Histoire de la danse en Occident*.

Beauchamp's work aspired to a moral and aesthetic ideal,[4] the pursuit of pure lines soaring upwards towards the sky, towards the inaccessible beyond, towards what was usually described as paradise.

But this was an artificial world in which nature became unrecognisable, in which gestures did not have their proper meaning and whose approach consisted of taking a natural movement and pushing it to its maximum development, thus rendering it artificial. Virtuosity and formal beauty were privileged to the detriment of substance.

> "The grand jeté was originally a lengthwise jump...The movement of dance was the idealisation of this natural jump: it had to convey the essence of the jump which was the freedom from gravity. Logically everything had to be conceived in order to give the impression of lightness which transformed the beauty of the gesture.
>
> The legs are stretched...The body is upright without being stiff, the arms are extended...The head rests straight on the torso where, the height of formalism, it is turned towards the audience. A magnificent figure whose body becomes weightless and whose every appearance of effort is completely erased". (Paul Bourcier)
>
> Classical dance is the perfect interpretation of a culture permeated over the centuries by Christian morality. "Classical dance inscribes Christian dogmas on the body".[5]

The discipline imposed on the body represents an asceticism whose object is to wrench man from the ground and from gravity.

> "Always taller on demi-pointe and on the very point of the foot, the dancer is in a glorious struggle with the effects of gravity".[6]

Classical dance designed the vertical. It remains a living image of the ideal of the Judeo-Christian soul symbolised by the cathedral spires which soar vertically through space towards the sky, the seat of God, according to the established religions.

This is shown by maintaining the body in an upright posture: the foot is arched, the knees are hyperextended, the backside is drawn in, the stomach is flat, the chest is held in, the vertebral column is rectilinear, the neck is stretched upwards.

Other dance styles seen in the West

The cult of classical dance and its points, so contrary to nature, dominated of the

---

4 The ballets of this period have no national roots and were created from stories and themes which had no basis in reality.
5 Pierre Legende, *La passion d'être un autre*.
6 Nancy Midol, "Danse Moderne".

nineteenth century.

The beginning of the twentieth century, on the other hand, was the age of "revolution" in the arts. The search for different horizons and different sources of inspiration existed in every creative spirit. It is possible that this condition had been inspired by the conquest of non-European territories, particularly in Africa, at the end of the preceding century and which resulted in greater knowledge of the culture of these countries.

The discovery of African arts and particularly African sculpture had a rejuvenating on European arts.

Modern dance

Twentieth century modern dance marked a rebirth. Man wanted to rediscover nature, to measure reality against himself. It was the unity of man and the earth, in rhythm with the cosmos. It was the expression of life but it only existed when it expressed attachment to a culture.

The evolution of modern dance in the West was achieved by Isadora Duncan who symbolised the freedom of her native America while returning to the sources of ancient Greece. Martha Graham also illustrated this attachment to American culture but she reintroduced the importance of percussion in dance. Laban rediscovered the importance of the natural milieu and its influence on dance. For him the origin of dance was in work.

Others, for example Doris Humphrey, created a dance form which struggled against gravity and tried to express man's search for equilibrium.

By contrast, the other great contemporary names, such as Merce Cunningham created "abstract" dances.

However, twentieth century western dance, on the whole, rediscovered the powerful lines of traditional African dance: unity with the cosmos, the importance of environment and freedom of execution.

Opposite:

This sculpture, with the arms and legs in dooplé, is a perfect illustration of the traditional African criteria of beauty. A curving line marks the eyes, the neck is long, the legs are bow-shaped, the whole body is rounded.

The vertical line on the head is the djiba gbole (an obligatory initiation for those who want to join the ranks of responsible men). It separates the front of the head into two parts (male and female) whose union leads to birth.

Montol sculpture, Nigeria, Annamel Gallery.

Chapter One
African Culture and the West

The first western contact with African culture came about through the navigators who brought back sculptures, often of ivory, from their voyages along the west coast of Africa. One receipt dating from 1470 attests to the purchase of an African statuette by Charles the Bold and during the Renaissance a captain from Dieppe, Jean Ango, showed some African black statuettes to Francis I.

But the real discovery of the different African countries visited by the European navigators dates from the second half of the seventeenth century: sculptures of the period from lower Zaire which featured in the collection of curiosities assembled in Rome by Athanasius Kircher.[1]

In 1686 the geographer Olfert Dappert gave a detailed account of the various African countries visited by the navigators of the period. For the first time ritual scenes were described in a book which brought a new dimension to the sculptures which were already known: magical, political, therapeutic and religious.[2]

But apart from the European traders who were established on the coasts, Africa remained unexplored and ignored by Europe. But by the end of the nineteenth century European expansionist ambitions were concentrated on the discovery of Africa and each new expedition became a kind of theatre.[3]

Evidence also emerged about the people who had been seen by these explorers. In the second half of the nineteenth century more than a hundred ethnographical objects had been brought back to Europe by the shipping companies and were given to the Museum of Natural History. The Museum of Man, founded in 1938, also testified to the growing interest in the arts of other continents.

For western art, the first decade of the twentieth century was one of the richest, most daring and most receptive to the art of other continents. The beginning of the century was characterised by a spirit of inquiry, a new look on the world, the need to make a *tabula rasa* of everything conventional that had gone before. It was the period in which Groddeck, the father of psychosomatics, explained to his patients

---

1 According to the recent work by Father Joseph Cornet, it seems that the sculptures from the Kircher Museum were not part of the original collection. *The Four Moments of the Sun*, Thompson and Cornet, Shnigto, 1981.
2 *Description de l'Afrique*, Olfert Dappert, Amsterdam, 1686, French translation.
3 In 1884-85 the Congress of Berlin partitioned the continent between the great powers. For some countries there was a later partition between 1905 and 1908.

the influence of the mind on the health of the body, and in which Sigmund Freud highlighted the instinctive aspect of human beings, affirming the pre-eminence of emotions and feelings, especially unconscious urges.

Artists discovered the primitive arts which satisfied their love of novelty. In order to escape from convention and to justify their own personal approach, they created a new style and the primitive arts supplied them with this novelty in the form of "tradition".

It was Matisse who discovered African art in 1906 and disseminated it among his friends in the modern movement: Picasso, Vlaminck, Derain, Juan Gris, Modigliani, Braque, L'Hote, Salmon, also Apollinaire and many others.[4] Cubism derived its inspiration from the art of African sculpture which was widely known throughout Europe.[5]

> "The negro masks open up a new horizon for me; they enabled me to make contact with things which are instinctive, direct expressions which oppose that false tradition which I detested". (Braque, 1915)

Although the first reactions to African art were negative (the masks were rejected as "grimacing" and the statuettes as "obscene"), fashion soon changed and there were many enthusiasts for this kind of provocative painting and sculpture in the "primitivism" movement.

Gradually interest in these new pictorial concepts grew and gallery owners displayed these daring works.[6]

After the First World War, the craze for jazz and the dances inspired by the descendants of North American slaves brought from America was a perfect reflection of the "Roaring Twenties". Wealthy connoisseurs began to collect African sculptures and did not bother too much about their provenance.[7] However there were a few Europeans who were suspicious of the peculiar character of these statuettes:

> "For several years artists, connoisseurs and museums have increased the interest in idols from Africa and Oceania but from a purely artistic point of view, making an abstraction of

---

4 Recent research by scholars such as William Rubin, Jean Louis Pauchat and Philippe Peltier argue that the artists of the period were not as influenced by black art as has been claimed and that most of the objects which were supposed to have inspired them were unknown in Europe.

5 The single example of the Congo is instructive. A study published in 1899 indexed the ethnographical collections of the Congo Museum and listed more than twenty thousand Congolese objects in various European museums. Thus there were 7549 Congolese objects at the Tervueren Museum, 3000 in Leiden, 2800 in Berlin, 1200 at the Trocadero in Paris, 600 in the British Museum and at Christiania (Oslo), 400 in Copenhagen etc.

6 Paul Guillaume was one of the first to defend the new art.

7 During the 1920s certain African sculptures were prized more than a painting by Modigliani or Sisley. Today connoisseurs are looking particularly for central African sculptures whose prices rival those for the Impressionists. It is impossible to ignore the existence of primitive art and its influence on contemporary art.

the supernatural character which was given to them by their original artists. But there is no critical apparatus for such a novel curiosity, and negro masks cannot be displayed in the same way as a collection of objets d'art (painting, statues) created in Europe or in the classical civilisations of Asia, Egypt and the other populated regions of North Africa".[8]

Apollinaire's preface is still relevant more than half a century later, in spite of ethnographers' studies and their attempts to locate African works in the milieu which created them and to explain their functions, their utility and their symbolic value.[9]

This persistent ignorance of African art in its numerous forms is due mainly to the oral African tradition and the absence of any written documents.

Unlike Asians or Westerners, Africans do not have a written tradition. This may be due to a number of reasons: the great variety of languages, the large number of tribes, the inability to construct writing materials suitable to the climate, the difficulty of preserving documents, the way of life, etc. The reason for this lack of written tradition matters little, it is a simply a fact. For twentieth century Africans there are no early written works to tell them about the imagination and history of their ancestors.

African "memory" exists in other and more varied forms. It slightly resembles a puzzle: it is impossible to recognise the exact meaning of one part without reconstructing it in full.

In the same way it is impossible to understand the significance of an African object, statuette or mask simply by looking at them because, for example, the apparent meaning of the object (its function) is complemented by the name [10] (its common designation) which comprises its particular symbolism.

Because verbal language is imperfect, it has to be complemented by the language of gesture which is more universal. The method and the time when this object is utilised conveys a different kind of information and gives it another significance.[11]

To Africans, statues and statuettes represent memory inscribed in form, the materialisation of knowledge from every sphere of life: practical, magical, therapeutic, divinatory.

They represent both memory and a teaching manual for choreographers and traditional African dancers just as they also illustrate the main basic movements of African dance. Thanks to these and to the oral memory transmitted by earlier generations, choreographers can design in space the invisible forms which have their roots in the everyday life of yesterday and today.

---

8 Guillaume Apollinaire, Preface to *Premier Album de Sculptures Nègres*, Paris, 1917.

9 Traditional African dance remains largely unknown to critics, choreographers and specialists in African art. To my knowledge there exists no study of the close links between African sculpture and traditional African dance.

10 The name is itself constructed of many elements each having a meaning on several levels. Thus dooplé (course, mortar), see p. 50.

11 A Westerner is unable to recognise the true meaning of a collar, a belt or a drum, regarding these objects as merely "African". The symbolic language of the object (see p. 86, the dancing objects) is part of African oral culture.

Chapter Two

Traditional African Dance

"I remember that when I went to tell my mother about my first success in the baccalaureat", writes Leopold Senghor, "she did not speak, she did not cry, she did not weep. She began to dance, slowly and gracefully, her face shining with joy".

Because it has more power than gesture, more eloquence than words, more richness than writing and because it expresses the most profound experiences of human beings, dance is a complete and self-sufficient language. It is the expression of life and of its permanent emotions—joy, love, sadness, hope—and without emotion there is no African dance.

Because dance involves emotion and induces an experience which cannot be conceptualised or reduced to words, the term dance, in many African languages, is only applied to human movements and not, as in the West, to those of animals.

According to the Robert dictionary, dance is "an expressive series of movements of the body executed according to a rhythm, and most often to the sound of music, and following an art, a technique or a social code which is more or less explicit".

This definition, however accurate, fails to mention the two conditions essential to African vision of dance freedom and awareness: freedom because the dancer must be free to dance or not and any dance performed under duress is not regarded as a dance by Africans. Thus the slaves who had no choice whether to dance or not, were not really dancing in the eyes of their people because there was neither joy nor a deep commitment on their part. Awareness because every real dance is an expression, it tells something and speaks to the heart of the spectator. Dance

---

Opposite

"In the beginning was the Dance and the Dance was in the Rhythm and the Rhythm was Dance", said Serge Lifar. The African child who is still suckling learns about rhythm and dance even before it can walk. Carried by its mother, it continues, as in the womb, to live with her rhythm and participates in the daily life of the village and in the dancing.

The mother is in dooplé, her breasts "have drunk the cup of contentment", a criterion of beauty in Africa. In African art this is the only depiction of maternity to be conceived in two parts. The cord which ties the child to the mother symbolises the dile or fibre of tree bark which carries the child on the back. The smaller cords around the waist have a mystic role; they symbolise the pee, a cord made from a mixture of palm fibre, incense and palm oil, representing as a circle the silver cord which ties man to God. This is also the image of the concentric circles and the infinite love of God.

Wooden Teke statuette (Congo). Height: 20.2cm. Rene Lehuard Collection.

something inexpressible; it is another form of expression. It is the link
₁ the body, the earth and the sky.
:e is the tangible proof of man's repeated endeavours to transcend himself.

Awareness and spirituality

The peculiarity of the African tradition is that it never makes an abstraction of nature
and cosmic laws, it gives the primary importance to the body, the necessary
intermediary without which spiritual life would be an abstraction.

African spirituality[1] starts from the principle that the only objective approach in
trying to encircle reality is through the body and that in rediscovering the body, one
rediscovers one's own identity in the midst of humanity and returns to it its rightful
place in the macrocosm.

In effect, this ascent to the centre of the macrocosm can only really be effected by
the descent to the microcosm which is represented by the body.

Human intelligence recognises the direct causes of things but cannot admit the
existence of forces which are beyond its comprehension. So long as the Ego is
dominant and does not abdicate before the grandeur and majesty of the cosmos,
human beings will never experience sincere religious feelings, they will not be able
to recognise a great mystic experience, they will not be able to make an experience
of those cosmic emotions which give meaning to life. Transcendental meditation,
the awareness of the universe, the experiences of the saints and the great mystics
cannot be achieved outside the body.

The strength of African tradition is that it draws its resources from the universe
and not from the narrow cult of reason.

To dance in the African manner is to recognise that man is inseparable from the
universe and that he is fundamentally a divine spark.

It also recognises that man does not have to be distorted by the essential things
in his life: his participation in the cosmos which proceeds from his participation in
the community.

It is the desire to know one's body, to live in the body, to obey it and its natural
experiences, in full awareness, without recourse to drugs. It is to have the courage
to respect laws which are not always those of logic, the irrational being one of the
privileged languages of the body.

It is also to have the courage of accepting pleasure. In African dance, relationships
are automatically charged with new meanings. Joy and happiness are the bonds
conveying feelings which are simultaneously more pure, noble and spiritual.

African dance also considers it a duty to "treat your own person as well as the
person of others, never simply as a means but always as an end". (Kant)

---

1   What is spirituality if not to feel within oneself the flow of energies and to be conscious of the
    vegetative currents which circulate in order to transcend them.

The Cou and the Zou

For an African, dance is a perfect manifestation which comes from the intimate union of cou and zou.

The cou is the term which defines the body of the dancer when he executes the dance: it is the public part of the dance.

The body of the African dancer overflows with joy and vitality, it trembles, vibrates, radiates, it is charged with emotions. Whatever the physical aspect of the dancer—thick or enormous, round or svelte, weak or muscled, large or small—as soon as his emotions are not repressed and stifled, as soon as the rational does not impose itself on him but accepts a collaboration with the irrational which is the true language of the body, the body becomes joyous, attractive, vigorous and magnetic. There emanates a beauty, a divine light blinding in its purity which bursts forth and radiates all the cells, illuminating everything around him, bringing calm and peace.

The zou is the abstract, conceptual part of dance. The term zou includes the determination of the dancer to dance, the freedom which he has to perform or not, his emotions and sensations and the different, involuntary aspects of the body.

Dance as the major component of African social life

In Africa dance is present everywhere, it is part of the daily life of the village and punctuates the main events of existence.

It is completely integrated into village activities and facilitates meetings and exchanges.

It is a privileged means of communication between human beings and allows them to express all their feelings and emotions.

When a child is born in a village, it is welcomed by the village with a dance. The inhabitants return to the fields at the news and "dance the news" on the spot, then return home, without even seeing the child. Is it a dance of gratitude or a dance of protection? It does not matter, it is a dance which marks the entry of the child into the life of the community.

THE TALENTS AND CULTURE OF TRADITIONAL AFRICAN DANCE

"Whether or not he is a musician, the African perceives the music of the interior. He lives with it, experiences it, plays it with an energy of which westerners are scarcely capable. The content of traditional African music is poetic because it is more animated. This is the way it must be approached and understood and not through that nauseating formula 'they have rhythm in their blood'". (Caroline Bourgine)

Dance is not a question of blood but of culture. Africans are not born with an extra dance chromosome and dance is no more instinctive for them than for other people.

The rhythm is neither African nor Brazilian, it is not the prerogative of certain peoples; it is universal because the rhythm is the beat of the heart.

African culture helps the early development of rhythm in the baby, perhaps because the baby is almost constantly carried by the mother.

The baby shares in all the movements of the mother while she is pregnant and in Africa mothers-to-be dance a lot. After the child is born it is pressed against the mother's back and experiences the daily life of the village with all its troubles and joys. Its life is cradled by the rhythms of life: walking, working and dancing.

But in every African village, there are people who never dance because they do not know how "to put one foot in front of the other" and I can confirm, as a dance teacher, that there are Africans who do not know how to dance.

Dance is a talent, like singing, painting or music. In the sphere of art, as elsewhere, talent is not everything. It has to be cultivated by work: Mozart spent eighteen hours a day at the piano; Marie Taglioni, a dancer of genius, forced herself to spend six hours a day practising.[2]

Africa has great dancers: these unknown geniuses help to demonstrate what this art acquires with a teacher, learns and masters over long years of work and practice, then transmits orally to new generations.

The Ignorance of traditional African dance

Traditional African dance as it is still practised today is the result of centuries of perfecting and cannot be understood or danced without training.

The Masques de Sagesse of West Africa who teach through the centuries' old oral tradition are the possessors and protectors of this dance knowledge and pass them on to initiates.

Unfortunately this teaching is unknown in the West because its rules are not written down and to many people African dancing is simply a matter of "shaking buttocks".

There are numerous so-called African dance courses in Europe but this teaching, which is useless, completely ignores the basic rules of the art.[3] This kind of course, which is popular with people who have an appetite for exoticism, are called "foufafou" by more sensible people and by the great African dancers. They teach only a certain egocentrism and although they sometimes help to release stiff bodies, they have absolutely no relationship with real African dance which has more spiritual aims and aspirations.

This ignorance of genuine African dance is mainly due to the absence of written documents and codified references. The teachers of these courses, who improvise

---

Opposite
Woman giving birth. This sculpture shows the omnipresence of dooplé in African life. Stiffness has no place even in birth. The mother lies naturally in dooplé.

Bamileke statuette, Cameroon. Maud and Rene Garcia Collection.

---

2 She devoted two hours a day to about a thousand exercises for each foot, two hours to balances or adagio and two hours to jumps.
3 One cannot be a teacher of African dance simply because one has a sense of rhythm.

for the most part, do not "know"; they have not been trained by the African Masques and are thus unaware of the basis of their teaching. If the spectators—critics or students—have no African background, they will be unable to relate to it or to differentiate between dancing "foufafou" and traditional dancing.

In the West, culture is largely based on writing and African dance lacks this method of dissemination. It was through written sources that dance won its public. The theoretical studies revealed the philosophy, techniques and basic movements; it "popularised" the knowledge of dance and "raised the cultural standard of the public in understanding and appreciation"[4]. In effect, as soon as dance became the subject of theoretical study, it spawned its own literature and developed because it was technically enriched by the relationship with the written word.

The absence of documentary sources on traditional African dance has hindered its expansion in the West and today every Western spectator of African dance is above all a non-African whose knowledge of dance is influenced, either consciously or unconsciously, by classical dance.

The national African ballet companies who make extensive western tours have helped to publicise an image of African dance in Europe. But mostly they are not understood by the spectators who have no way of judging them.

It is also true that dancers of African origin adapt themselves to their audiences and their dance becomes less African in character. Some of the more well-known ones are culturally more Western than African.

The expressive African dance of Elsa Wolliaston

Elsa Wolliaston left her native Kenya for England when she was sixteen. She then went to America before settling in France in 1969. "I worked with Frank Wagner, Merce Cunningham...The explosion in my artistic life took place not in Africa but in America and Europe", she says.

The richness and variety of her cultural cross-breeding helped her to achieve performances which are Western in concept and construction but which correspond to the criteria of Western dance and beauty.

Wolliaston's talents are known and appreciated in Europe but are practically unknown in Africa and have little connection with traditional African dance. Dancers, choreographers and spectators—mostly Western—rediscover their own culture; they understand and appreciate what they see because the references are more Western than African.

African dance in the West

The experience of the Guinean Ammed Tidjani Cisse is different. He chose to abandon the legal career which seemed destined for him after a brilliant school career in order to dance. He has directed the Grands Ballets d'Afrique in Paris since

---

4   Hindu dance was more privileged in this respect because all the steps and gestures of Hindu dance were codified in the Natya Sastra.

1976.

When he arrived in France Cisse knew how to dance in the African sense of the term and he had enough material to create an African ballet. He also knew how to pass these on to others.

In Cisse's ballets the body of each individual in the corps de ballet becomes a universal body, projected into the cosmos, in close communion with the fauna, flora, stars and mountains—an infinite body, limitless.

Like the great African ballets, his works produce dancers who perpetuate the gestures and the living dances of the centuries. They are living choreographic and musical museums.

However, Cisse's ballets have created little interest among Western audiences. The silence surrounding his work is due to the ignorance of the media and the public about the true language of original African dance.

Mudra Afrique or getting to know African dance

Maurice Béjart, whose father, the philosopher Gaston Berger, was Franco-Senegalese, has attempted to forge a bridge between African and classical dance. He wanted African dance to gain recognition through its own particular character so that it can take its rightful place in modern civilisation. He wanted "to give Africa faith in its own dance and to continue its human integration through dance in the midst of an invasive technology which though necessary is often destructive".

This led to the founding of Mudra Afrique in 1977 in Dakar, with the support of many organisations, though it was also a failure.

The aim of Mudra Afrique was an attractive one: "to take root in the values of black consciousness in order to be open to the values of other cultures…To achieve a new black African dance which will be experienced and enjoyed by people of all civilisations because it is part of the universe". (Senghor)

However these values had no clear objective. There was no previous study or research on the specific nature of traditional African dance, one of the primary black African values on the artistic level.

The admission requirements for Mudra Afrique have more to do with the needs of western theatre dance than with the imperatives of traditional African dance.[5]

At Mudra Afrique there was everything except Africa. The school eventually had to close mainly through lack of money but also because its ignorance of African culture meant that it was ill-equipped to realise its aims.

African culture exists, it lives. But it is impossible to graft arbitrarily onto it a conception of art which does not conform to its own values.

African dance is the repetition of gesture learned according to tradition. This does not mean simple imitation or copying of the teacher but a complete knowledge of gesture which leaves the dancer free within the technique to improvise and respond through gestures which, according to his inspiration, are part of the call of the

---

5   Birago Diop's *Cumba* which was created at Dakar included choreographic figures from classical dance. The African audience (apart from the elite) regarded it as a theatre piece, not dance.

cosmos.

The traditional African dancer is in perpetual dialogue with the cosmos and as in every language he respects the "words" but he also improvises and creates his own "phrase".

> "The language of learned gesture constitutes the statement accepted by the consensus of the group whose dance master is the authority…each dancer who has acquired this skill through repetition is permitted to differentiate his own statement from those of the other members of the group…"

This is the essence of real, traditional African dance: continual improvisation and creation, constantly renewed from within a well-defined group. To compare it to a stagnant lake is to ignore its profound nature and African culture as a whole.[6]

Traditional African dance and mime

Traditional African dance, revealed and passed on by the Masques and the Elders (Anciens) during ceremonies, is evidence of the respect of man for the universe. And because it does not reflect daily life but is rather the materialisation of man's attempt to "express" feelings in a more genuine way, it does not use mime. This is because the gestures and attitudes of mime tend to reproduce exact reality and to arouse feelings by exaggerating facial expressions to the point of caricature.

Thus there is no mime in traditional African dance and if it ever did appear it would constitute an impoverishment, reducing African dance to the level of a simple copy of reality.

The dances, whether beo or gnenon,[7] offer villagers the possibility of externalising their emotions and aspirations to a higher world. But dance is and should be a universal language, and in order to be understood by all it should respect the codes known to all. This is the reason why traditional dance is taught and learned. The basic movements, gestures, attitudes and positions are learned. Only after this is improvisation possible.

INNOVATION, IMPROVISATION AND CREATIVITY

Africans tend to be uninterested in any art which lacks improvisation. Sculptors, minstrels, singers, percussionists, dancers, poets and painters—all are conscious of this fact.

Every innovation and creation involves a thorough knowledge of technique which can then be "forgotten" in order to allow spontaneous personal variations.

True creativity only really exists when it is part of dancing. In every traditional

---

6 "Tradition should not be a lake of stagnant water but an impetuous torrent which rushes into the modern world in order to overturn it". Maurice Béjart

7 See p. 29.

African dance the dancer is free to improvise because traditional African dances depend both on the repetition of basic movements and on improvisation around those movements. This is its superiority.

This type of improvisation enables the dance teacher to appreciate quickly the standard of knowledge of his student because the gestures of the dancer soon become repetitive, revealing his sense of rhythm, his capacity to coordinate his movements and his perception of space and style.

The new must be born from the old

This African law, which exists in dance as much as in sculpture, has given birth to various interpretations. Improvisation in Africa is not a result, as in the West, of spontaneity but much more of the creative imagination of the improviser who applies himself to a given subject known to everybody. The spectators judge it as connoisseurs. The improviser must never lose sight of the canvas of his subject. He must improvise on that or on the basic movements of the dance. It can be argued that the work of improvisation is determined by the structure of the basic movements of the dance which is performed.

The dancer can "paraphrase" each of the principal basic movements whose enchainment constitutes the totality of the dance, that is, that he can exploit these to the maximum, amplify and magnify them. But he can also improvise in such a way that the totality of basic movements plays both the role of the canvas on which he works, and that of refrain, during which he rests and takes a breath.

Collective improvisation by dancers in the same group or in the same village is a form of improvisation completely ignored in the West.

This form of improvisation is disconcerting, so disconcerting that it passes completely unnoticed by the spectators who are not initiated into real African dance. On the other hand, for the Elders and the connoisseurs, this form is the most refined and the most enjoyable. As in the primary form of improvisation, the dancers do not move any way they want, they take account both of the basic movement of the dance they perform and of the action of their partners.

The dance steps serve as a spring-board and a guard-rail in the same way that the basic theme serves as a benchmark for the singers[8] of the orchestra which accompanies the Masques de Sagesse.

In collective improvisation there is a reflex which leads one dancer to execute the gesture suitable to complement the movement of another dancer. Unconsciously it establishes a current, an immediate communion between the dancers.

In order to practise collective improvisation correctly there are certain rules which must be observed:

— The dancers must be used to dancing in a group (theatre groups have the advantage here of being more regular and stable).

---

8 They also improvise and know each other's role, just as jazz musicians know the parts which they have to play.

— To master the dances completely in order to excel in the basic movements.

— To have a good sense of rhythm in order to play with the music, while remaining in unison with the partners.

— To appeal to the direct perception of the number or simply to the numeric sensation[9] in order to determine in advance the stops and the calls of the principal percussionist whose action always affects the dancers in the course of improvisation.

— Finally, and most important, the dancer must love dancing.

The author's experience

Dabou is a small town on the banks of the Ebrie lagoon, in the south of the Ivory Coast. It is the town of my youth, my dreams, my hopes and my memories. The evocation of its name awakes in me a certain nostalgia which always catches in my throat.

In Dabou I learned how to read, write and count. It is where I had my first successes at school. At Dabou my brothers and sisters were born. Dabou, Dabou…

In 1957 we lived in a small house, invisible in the middle of tall grass, at the very heart of the town which was the capital of the Adioukrou. This sinister grass, which we called Bin, had to be cut very often so that it would not swamp us. It also had to be cut in order to protect us from the animals which hid in the grass and this created a lot of work for my father.

One day my father said to me: "My son, from now on you will cut this grass every Thursday". I always hated manual work and the idea of having to cut this grass every Thursday, although it only took fifteen minutes, did not please me at all, especially since it was time taken away from football.

Nevertheless, on the first Thursday I cleared a piece of land as well as I could. The following Thursday, since I had not cut the grass to ground level as my father had done and since it had rained a lot during the week the grass had grown on the piece of land I had not cleared. It looked as if nothing had been done for two weeks.

Faced with this embarrassing situation I began to seek a solution which would enable me to overcome the grass without having to bend down the whole time and I arrived at the conclusion that somehow it was essential to stop the grass from growing and surrounding our yard and our house.

The following days I suddenly had an idea: I would get on top of a cask (or an empty barrel) and make it roll with my feet, supporting myself with a stick of bamboo or wood. The stick made a kind of paddle which helped me to roll the cask and a cane with which to support myself while balancing on the cask.

Admittedly the beginning was difficult and, despite my stick, I immediately fell every time that the cask began to roll. But gradually things were sorted out and I was able to crush all the grass. The work even became a kind of game. First I learned

---

9   This aptitude has nothing to do with abstract counting, which relates to a more complicated mental phenomenon constituting a recent acquisition of human intelligence.

how to balance myself on the cask while making it roll quickly. Then one day I abandoned the stick and used only the force of my feet—in particular the underside of my toes—to make the cask move forward.

From that day on I had a crowd of spectators every Thursday and the work, so tedious at the beginning, became agreeable and stimulating. Moreover the grass did not reappear since the almost constant presence of the crowd had completely smothered it.

One day I decided to change the terrain and to roll the cask over earth which was dry and hard. This considerably increased the speed of my "engine" as well as the risks of accident. Then I initiated my friends into my art and arranged courses. This new aspect of the game created a great feeling of comradeship and increased the number of participants. After that, competitions took place every Thursday under the admiring gaze of our supporters.

After that I stepped up the difficulty and went from dry, hard terrain to a gently sloping incline which was just enough to triple the speed of my cask. This was successful.

One day I heard the percussion of the Goumbe[10] and began to perform some basic steps on top my cask while it was rolling. Later, spurred by the drums and their intoxicating rhythms, I achieved several relatively complex figures such as jumping and falling back on the cask while it rolled with mad speed.

This early experience opened up all the great pleasures and constraints of dance, in a spirit of rigour for itself and respect for others.

It also illustrated on a microscopic scale how dance could reproduce the needs and imperatives of daily life.

---

10 A popular dance in West Africa.

Gnenon dance at Vogan, Togo, April 1966.

The female dancers are quite old. The others, in the circle, make the pou pou slapping their mouths with their hands at regular intervals. These sounds aim to invoke and evoke the gods of dance and festivals but they also help the women to render homage to them.

Chapter Three
The Influence of the Natural World

In the conception and evolution of dances, it is important to emphasise the role of the natural world.

The environment of a human being influences his behaviour. Unconsciously the human being adapts his way of life and his dances to the surroundings in which he lives.

MOUNTAINS

The mountain man lives in a world of hills and steep slopes, jagged and rocky, in which he has little room to move: his approach is one of prudence.

In general he breeds animals and lives among his sheep, goats and livestock who have agile feet in order to root out the tufts of grass growing on the rocks. His bearing is brisk, and in imitation of the animal world which surrounds him he can also leap from rock to rock.

Because he has to travel many miles a day, he is supple. In order to climb he carries his body weight either on the front part of the soles of his feet or on his toes.

Finally he is always looking towards the heights.

The mountain dances have their own particular character because, as they have little space, the dancers cannot perform all the dances. The dances are animated and alert, they are danced in place, with height. There are a lot of jumps and leaps.

The principal, basic movements are a sequence of dooplé, zépié, kagnioulé and a rigorous soumplé.

Thus the Simbos in the mountainous region of Ivory Coast have airy dances in which the dancers are thrown in the air and caught in the arms.[1]

THE PLAIN

Unlike the mountain people, the people of the plains are peasants who cultivate a few acres of fertile land. The countryside is rich and flat, everything grows in

---

1 The "ländler", the folkloric dance of the Bavarian Alps in Germany, have the same aerial exercises.

abundance and there is ample space.

The eyes are lowered towards the ground which they clear, sow and harvest. Their approach is slow and steady, they carry their body weight on the whole of the soles of their feet. They learn to walk on the tips of their toes in order to approach snares around the circular fences of wood or bamboo which they have constructed to protect the produce from dangerous animals.

Because they have access to so much space, the plains people can "waste" space. The dances are more varied and more near to the earth, there are rounds (sahan) in which the dancers move from one place to another, races or farandoles.

Since they are not restricted, plains dancers perform every kind of step and use every basic movement.

THE FOREST

The man of the virgin forest lives by hunting and gathering in a world of gigantic trees with luxuriant foliage and undergrowth of firm but spongy soil, with a scattering of branches, brambles and bushes. His legs are accustomed to movements of flexing and stretching because he is often obliged to move on all fours, to bend, to squat or to jump over water courses or tree trunks which obstruct his way. His bearing is thus slow, alert and prudent.

As a good hunter he is compelled to walk gently and slowly in order to surprise his prey. He has to know how to place his foot on dry branches without snapping them, to trample on ground strewn with dead leaves without making noise and to walk through water without attracting the attention of the animals which drink there.

He is armed with spears, bows and formidable arrows. He has to raise himself on the tips of his toes in order to see better, or in order to reach the berries or the fruits on the trees.

But he is also obliged to keep on the look-out for game at all hours and in all positions, stretched out on his back, his stomach or his side or sitting comfortably, bending on his knees, squatting or in dooplé. Thus his dances are near the ground.

The very active life of the forest man predisposes him to dances which are both lively and slow because he is strong and supple. Because he knows how to utilise the point of his foot to absorb his body weight, to aim his bow and to gather fruits, his dances are also airy and light.

THE COAST

The man of the coast knows the privilege of the sea and its riches. His fisherman's hut is built at the edge of the sea on golden, sandy beaches. He knows nothing about farming the soil of the plains or the mountains, while walking makes extra demands on him because of the sand which slips through his feet at every step.

His bearing is very particular and difficult. In order to avoid getting bogged down, he has perfected a technique which consists of walking by placing the sole of the foot as flat as possible while making every effort to lighten the body weight.

His dances are less varied but more rigorous, precise and more technically refined.

He dances placing his feet as flat as possible, one after the other, with determination and a restrained strength. Since the use of the feet is restricted, he uses the torso, shoulders and the head to complement his dance.

The agbaza is a traditional dance from the Benin coast. The dancer is in dooplé (flexed knees), the arms partly folded on the chest; he executes a series of movements beginning with the shoulders and the shoulder blades. Always in dooplé, his feet pound the earth in turn.

In the gazo, a traditional dance from the coast of Togo, the placement of the arms is the same although the feet, instead of beating the earth, glide successively backwards, before returning in dooplé.

The coastal man is often a fisherman and his dance reflects his way of life. Standing or sitting in his canoe, the fisherman is constantly in dooplé. Whether he

Malicondi, a territorial dance from Dajaon, Togo, March 1971. This coastal dance has steps which relate to the difficulty of walking on the sand. The thighs are in soumplé, the arms in naou or nai, suggesting wings and feathers. The torso, as always in African dance, inclines lightly towards the front. The gaze is fixed toward the ground. Everything about the dancer suggests effort. The drummer concentrates all his attention on the feet of the dancer.

The dancer's headdress has an initiation function, like the cords which entwine his shoulders and form circles.

paddles or whether he casts his net, the strength of his body in movement comes from the equilibrium which makes his legs flexed.

His hips dance, his chest vibrates, the breast twists to the right or to the left according to the gesture, his shoulders swing, fall and shake, the head moves, the whole body undulates to the will of the waves.

Walking in sand and the constant search for equilibrium on board the canoe makes the man of the coast the incontestable master of every dance which requires vibrations of the torso, the chest, the shoulders and the head while beating the ground.

The observation of men in their natural surroundings enables us to understand how man has always attempted to rise on the point of his foot, not for spiritual or metaphysical reasons but for practical reasons.

However, Africans have never adopted the use of points in dance because they are unnatural and because they are opposed to the philosophy of African dance which tends to a high level of technique while preserving a great respect for the body. They prefer to use stilts to grow tall.

Traditional African dance on stilts or the African way to dance on point while respecting the body

Stilts almost certainly originated with the forest man who, wishing to gather fruits which were too high up to pick, thought not of lengthening their arms by means of a pole which would throw them off balance, but of lengthening their legs by going up on stilts, thus gaining in balance, time and energy. This was not achieved at once but by patience and perseverance. The dance on stilts is the confirmation of this long effort.

This dance, which can be seen in the neolithic rock paintings of Tassili, is found today in many African countries: Togo, Ivory Coast, Guinea, Benin, Gabon, Mali, Cameroon, Angola, Liberia.

It has been claimed that stilts dances were a guarantee of fertility and that the big steps were "a motif running through dances of growth" and that this was "the elongation of steps which one would have primitively sought through the use of stilts" in order to shorten the time between sowing and harvest.[2]

The mystic law which every African knows is: "Ask of the cosmos what you wish but do not impose any solution. Never demand of the cosmic forces what you think is owed to you".[3]

The mystic laws are founded on the inductive reasoning of experimental science and every dancer or teacher of African dancing versed in metaphysical sciences is aware of this strictness.

To suggest to God in a dance that he shorten the time between the harvest (representing this shortening through big steps on stilts) is to impose a solution on God and thus violates a mystical law which is not authentically African.

---

2   Curt Sachs quoted by Jacques Bernolles.
3   The very fact of asking God for a solution automatically invalidates all other possibilities.

Moreover, the dances which are performed in order to communicate with the cosmic forces, such as the dances of growth, are lively and joyful, their rhythm throbbing and vibrant.[4] While praying to God, the dancer is moving. Technically, it is almost impossible to perform fast dances[5] in the same way as those on stilts. "What we gain in length, in the size of the steps, in extension, we lose in power", states a technical authority on African dance.

Dances on stilts were the idea of an African dance master in order to get round the obstacles posed by the tradition and attitude very prevalent in Africa but above all in the area of art.[6]

Tradition forbids the use of points, a position declared to be unnatural by the Elders[7] because it does not respect the body (they claim that the excessive use of points can lead to madness or mental unbalance). However, the use of stilts is not prohibited.

The stilt walker does not seek balance but rather explores the limits of balance.

Gueblin and Gueguia of the Yacouba (in western Ivory Coast), the stilt walkers of Benin or those of the national ballet of Togo perform various feats: a series of perilous exercises accomplished with suppleness and skill, high jumps, whirling around on one leg.

> "Suddenly Gueblin appears. He emerges from the forest preceded by a guide who leads him through the dance. He is over nine feet tall. His face is hidden by a mask of black cloth which is extended to a conical head-dress decorated with shells. There are coverings (rather like trousers) on the legs and the stilts and a skirt of raffia is fixed to the tail.
>
> When Gueblin dances, the percussion players and singers redouble their efforts. Like a fine, great elegant bird, the stilt walker manoeuvres himself. He fills the space, turns, whirls round and "takes flight". He is only in the air for a second but the spectator has the impression that his flight lasts for much longer. His guide and helpers surround him in order to cushion any fall. The cries are piercing but then everything is calm. He falls back, standing, arms wide apart. He has really taken flight".[8]

It is incorrect to say that the stilt walkers were representations of spirits or

---

4 They are part of what are called action dances: those of conquest, fighting, freedom and independence.
    In music and dance, Africans express success, the beauty of life, good fortune and rejuvenation through a great consumption of energy and vivacity. They deploy these virtuoso talents. By contrast, everything slow and monotonous expresses sadness and grief.

5 Little steps are necessary in traditional African dance in order to realise the beauty and complexity of the play of the legs. They allow the dancer to perform quickly and they give the impression of dancing with energy while beating the earth.

6 In order to realise a mask which respects the laws of the Elders, the anonymity of the wearer of the mask is usually protected. Although the eyes of the mask are represented by circles, one sculptor has skirted tradition by making the eyes tubular in shape for this particular mask. The law was preserved.

7 Tendonitis of the shins and knees ("jumper's knee") and the weakening of the tendons of the large fibula are the most common injuries in classical dance and the technical books on classical dance recommend plenty of caution and preparatory exercises.

8 Raoul Lehuard, *Arts d'Afrique Noire*.

The stilt dance of the Guebline Mask. Holding a bile (dancing object) in his hand, he balances on one leg, leaping into the air for a second.

The interpreters surround him, attentive to his slightest gestures. Since they are responsible to the Earth of the Mask (the image of God), they must see that no accident occurs during the dance. If the Mask drops, this is supposed to bring terrible misfortune for which they have to recompense the Society of Masks.

The principal percussion-player participates, calls out and improvises. He has complete osmosis with the dancer whom he complements perfectly. A second drummer plays the bass part throughout the whole dance. This bass part corresponds to dance steps which are specific to the dance being performed.

A Yacouba village of Godefouma, western Ivory Coast.

divinities living in the air, and that this dance was the result of an initiation of Africans by a protecting divinity.

To educated Africans the Mask comes from the bush or the forest. In certain civilisations, such as the Yacouba[9] the stilt walkers are thought to be spirits and they enjoy the same status as the bearers of the mask. On the other hand, there is no particular character accepted by the Kono of Guinea as completely inoffensive and amusing. This is true also of Siwere-were whose stilts are only three feet high, or the stilt walkers of Wogu, Manigri (Benin) or Tchamba (Togo).

BEO AND GNENON DANCES

The terms beo and gnenon signify respectively male and female and they are found in various forms all over Africa and with different standards regarding the concept of black African art.

In Kman or temple of the Oueon there are female masks with a smooth face and fine features, and male masks with a rough and distorted face. Among the Baoule of Ivory Coast, the Goli couple are eloquent examples of the beo and gnenon masks. In sculpture the beo objects always carry a handle while the gnenon always have a cavity so that the former can theoretically fit into each other in seconds.

African stories also illustrate this difference.

Among the Akye[10] there are male stories and female stories. One beo story of the Akye is called a journey, from beginning to end, without interruptions or songs, without any intervention by the audience. They remain passive and are content to reply with a simple "yes" to the narrative of the storyteller. The beo story is in fact a long monologue by the storyteller or by a griot (minstrel).

In contrast a gnenon story of the Aky always has a break. It has many phases and is accompanied by songs, percussion, melodies, a crash of voices, tongue-cluckings, clicks of the fingers, smiles and silences.

At the end of each phase the narrator stops his story and intones a poetic chant, immediately repeated by the chorus with the help of the audience. Then the narrator takes up his story again as far as the next phase whose secret he alone holds. He intones a new chant or repeats the preceding one.

Among the Oueon of the Ivory Coast there are two kinds of female stories. In the former the narrator proceeds exactly like the Akye; in the latter the narrator sings the story and the crowd takes up the refrain after each stanza. There is no conversation, everything is sung from beginning to end.

Beo Dances

A beo dance is a symbolic dance whose aim is to lead the dancer to communicate

---

9 Gueguia of the Yacouba uses an orchestra and an interpreter in order to direct him and attend to him while he enters.
10 The people of the Ivory Coast.

with God through the harmony of his body and spirit. Each gesture has its own meaning.

It is a dance with an initiating and spiritual character and has a specific name in the ethnic group which created it. It was an obligatory part of the early dances. It is performed with a rhythm of its own and involves a basic, precise movement which distinguishes it from other dances.

Thus a beo dance is a concrete dance, independent, initiating, refined over the centuries. It has a body, a soul and is self-sufficient with regard to rhythm, music and technique.

The teaching of beo dance is accompanied by theoretical instruction in the history of its symbolism and traditions.

Finally, it does not lend itself easily to improvisation. Only very fine dancers can improvise around the structured figures of the beo dance because all the positions and basic movements which comprise the enchainments of the dance have a precise role: to rouse a particular, psychic centre, to create a defined sensation and to stimulate a specific gland.

Gnenon Dances

A gnenon dance is above all a dance of entertainment, within the range of everybody, which allows the crowd to let themselves go during the great public events. They are crowd dances which do not need rigorous training unlike the beo dances. Individual expression, the picturesque and the natural are encouraged.

The gnenon dance is a dance of rejoicing, non-initiating which also has a specific name among the ethnic group which created it.

Consisting of simple elements, it can be performed with different music and rhythms and can include competitions in time and space. However, if it lasts a long time, it can perhaps become a beo dance although the reverse is impossible.

It lends itself very well to improvisation; fashionable dances created to modern music, the so-called creations of modern, contemporary African dance, those danced to African rhythms in night-clubs can all be included among gnenon dances. This is the kind of dance found most often in the West and on which traditional African dance is judged.

However, to an African knowledge of one or more gnenon dances does not confer the title of dancer.

Every course in African dance aimed at beginners must start with a thorough study of gnenon dances. The figures of several of these dances help the coordination of movement to develop. Moreover, the repetition of simple steps in a world of rhythmic music facilitates the acquisition and the skill of a sense of rhythm.

The performance of several gnenon dances can, occasionally, take the place of warm-up and training exercises before approaching the most difficult part of the programme. One good way of relaxing the students after class is to ask them to perform some gnenon dances with partial or complete freedom to express how they experience the music.[11]

---

11 The study of these kinds of dance is clearly not the same thing: the beo danses are studied in caillo or in gla, while gnenon dances are studied in glo. See p. 39.

Gomba, a beo or male dance from Mali. When learning this initiation dance (whose rules can never be changed) a caillo technique is imperative.

The dancers are in koou djiba in sahan, that is in a circle and on their knees. The dance has no meaning unless they hold the dancing objects which are personal to them. Any mistake in the execution of the dance is thought to bring misfortune to the dancer.

Chapter Four
The African Conception of the World

Africans are profoundly animist and thus they believe in reincarnation. The evolution of the personality through reincarnations is symbolised by a spiral and not by a straight line. In Africa the evolution of man is symbolised by a snail's shell.[1]

Curved lines, circles, cylinders—which to Africans are characterised by many circles of the same diameter piled one on top of the other—spirals, figures which have a helical or ellipsoid form are all integral parts of African culture. They faithfully reflect the habits and customs of this vast continent and one can find them in different aspects of life and in the global vision of the African world.

> "At the beginning is the point.
> This point extends along a curved line.
> This curve proceeds in conformity with the law.
> This law keeps the curve equidistant from the original point.
> And the curve while lengthening forms a circle.
> This circle is completed at a point called Sindrou which restricts its power of extension".

All the schools of initiation have as their primary aim to help man face the mysteries of life and their teaching relies on spiritual and scientific knowledge inherited from the ancient civilisations.

In the same way as the waves which advance freely in three directions often reshape the surroundings in which they extend their spreading front in the form of a geometric curve (circle, sphere. ellipsoid), so African spirituality is symbolised by three concentric circles, each corresponding to a different stage of spirituality:

— A very large circle symbolises the world, the village, the crowd or the body, and represents the most human and earthy stage. This is the world of simple human values.

— A second circle, inside the first, but more restricted, represents people of intellect, intermediaries, more detached from the world than those of the first circle but nevertheless partly integrated into this world. This is the world of the

---

1   The starting point for each new phase of the snail shell is either higher or lower than that of the preceding period. This gives an image of movement and evolution, and evokes the dance.

intellect, of the search for a more "spiritual" state;

— Finally, a third circle much smaller than the other two because, immediately surrounding the centre of the preceding circles, it symbolises the spiritual world. It is the world of the initiates, the Masques (Masks).

As the Africans see it, there is a continual crossing or exchange from one circle to the other because they cannot conceive of a world in which the fundamental facts are not a part of spirituality.

The privileged form of exchange between these three stages of spiritual evolution of man is dance, a medium common to each circle. We see that traditional African dance respects and illustrates this concept of the three concentric circles, as in other cultural spheres.

BELIEFS

Certain great Masques de Sagesse make their appearance at the age of seven, fourteen, twenty-one or older, according to their importance in the hierarchy of the world of the Masques, a veritable philosophical school whose oral teaching goes back to time immemorial.

Before returning to the world of the invisible, the masks carried by their interpreters or their servants draw a circle around the village within which they can be seen for the last time before they leave the material world for the time being.

During important ceremonies the great Masques de Sagesse always wait inside a circle traced with the ashes of palm leaves. The same happens with a new member, during the investitures of chiefs or the transfer of power.

The collars and belts which decorate the chiefs or the dancers during the dances of initiation evoke the circles and in sculptures of numerous masks one sees these three circles, especially as the openings for the eyes.[2]

The circle remains the basis of the prayers of the hunters to find a part of the forest with game.

THE CIRCLE IN ARCHITECTURE

The African village combines two types of organisation, one general, the other specific.

The architecture of the traditional African village was based on the circle but, replaced now by urban civilisation, this has tended to disappear.

Surrounded by a kind of circular fence, it comprised a large circle composed of

---

2 The bearer of a Masque de Sagesse must remain anonymous and cannot be recognised. When the face on a mask is being created the sculptor takes particular care with the eyes so that the bearer can see without being recognised. Thus some Masques have eyes in the form of a cylinder, a happy inspiration of the sculptor which respects two imperatives: the "magic" concentric circles and anonymity.

many round huts, the centre being represented by the dwelling of the traditional chief. The surrounding fence protects the village from the world of the hostile wild animal and the high palisades which protect the fields against dangerous beasts fit the shape of the fields and are generally circular.

Every family or group lives in an enclosed space. The round huts are constructed in circles which are drawn with the aid of rudimentary compass made of wood ends cut at right angles and string.

During meals the families sit in a circle around the dishes of food and so although the circle is certainly found in dance, it also occurs in every area of African life.

The cooking utensils also have curved lines. The pestle is rounded either at one or both ends while its handle is cylindrical. The mortar which plays a particularly important role in the life of the peasant is circular and its trunk has curved lines, its opening forms a circle and its base is circular.

In certain African regions the Kman or temple of the Masques de Sagesse is located a little outside the villages. The kman is rigorously composed of three concentric circles. The first circle, the most external, is made by a wall of palm leaves supported by trunks of wood and bamboo. The second circle is represented by the circular wall of the hut in which the most important initiations take place. The third circle is united with the centre of the hut and that of the palm leaf wall.[3]

SOCIAL LIFE

The basic education of each small African village depends on public speaking and it is no coincidence that many Africans are brilliant advocates.

The orator always argues while respecting the spiral scheme. He never refutes the statements of his adversary by a categorical negative but rather through a series of points which he develops spirally. This recalls the image of a spiral staircase or a snail shell. The language used is very colourful and abounds with rather baffling proverbs.

In the case of a dispute or misunderstanding between a couple of members of the same family, it is the council of judges and wise men who pass the verdict. Those who are in the wrong have to apologise publicly while tracing a circle drawn with fresh water around those who are in the right.

The customary rights of Africans are very strict but the laws have never been written down. Certain acts—somewhat similar to those forbidden under the Mosaic law—are automatically condemned by the whole society. But apart from these acts, the plaintiff and the defendant are on an equal footing and have just one method of persuasion: the art of debate. The plaintiff must prove the basis of his complaint while the defendant has to refute the statements of his adversary with his own arguments. It is an exercise in intellectual competence.

The lack of written texts and the slight quality of isolated proofs and testimonies always swing the balance in favour of those who have a better mastery of the

3   See p. 86 and Alphonse Tierou, *Verite premiere du second visage africain*, Maisonneuve et Larose, 1975.

techniques of pleading. When I was secretary to the famous customary chief Jean Babia of Adjame (an important area of Abidjan), I knew of cases in which those who appeared to have right on their side lost to those who were clearly in the wrong.

THE DANCE

African dance, the major component of African culture, also depends on the circle, the symbol of life which is both spiritual and temporal.

The arc of the circle or the circle itself is the spontaneous arrangement which the dancers, or the spectators around the dancers, take in the meeting place of the village.

The spectators symbolise the largest circle, the dancer represents the second circle, a necessary intermediary between the spectators and the spiritual aspect of the dance, a kind of "the spirit of the dance", an indispensable link in the dissemination of its intrinsic message.

But the dancer needs a large circle of villagers who will carry and assist him, helping him to surpass himself in order to reach the third circle and convey this message.

CRITERIA OF BEAUTY

The curve and the round are also the basic criteria of African beauty. The parts of the human body which constitute the true standards with which to evaluate the charm and beauty of a human being are, apart from the face, the neck, the breasts, the stomach, the legs and the buttocks.

The kind of neck which most pleases Africans is long, drawn up in front (like the neck of Nefertiti) and ringed, that is one whose natural folds are arranged in circles. Having such a neck is a quality much sought by African women. The straight neck, vertical and thick, is of no interest.

The sculpture emphasises in an eloquent way this concept of beauty over the whole of the continent. Women with long, ringed necks are found in the Dogon statues of Mali, the Yoruba Ekoi of Nigeria, the Senoufo, Baoule or Guere of Ivory Coast, the Fang Mashango of Gabon, the Bamileke and Ayang in Cameroon, the Mossi of Burkina Fasso, the Loulouwa of Zaire and are also seen on the combs of the Ashanti and the foot-stools of the Luba.

The breasts, well-rounded, harmonious, with curved lines only attracted the admiration of the Elders if they belonged to a young girl.

Drooping breasts signify that a woman has had children who have been nourished with mother's milk and are not regarded as either a physical or aesthetic embarrassment.

Among the Oueon, for example, the life of a woman can be divided into three sections:

Gninin an zoro dobo, "the breasts expect little brothers and sisters", marks the period from birth to puberty in which the breasts achieve their definitive form. The fact that the breasts grow one after the other has given rise to this expression which associates their development with the concept of fertility.

Gninin an von, "the breasts knock against each other" expresses the youth, the vitality, the size and above all the roundness of the breast ready to receive the baby for its milk.

Gninin an boulou, "the breasts begin to drink the cup of contentment" indicates the final condition of the African woman whose breasts have drooped after many pregnancies. This condition classes her among the responsible women who have the respect of old and young alike. It is an external sign of procreation which promotes the young woman to the status of doou (mother), the first in a series of honorific titles: doou of a whole family (in the sense of an extended African family), doou of a whole village, doou of a complete generation, doou of all the Masques de Sagesses.

In the first two phases of a woman's life, the nipples of her breasts point proudly towards the horizon, an image of youth searching for its ideal in the immensity of the cosmos. In the last phase the breasts abandon the horizon and are pointed towards the mother-earth. But whether she embraces the horizon or the earth with her protective and nourishing gaze, the charm of the female breast is derived from the African wisdom about its harmonious contour.

The abdomen. Africans are indifferent to a flat stomach. "Neither stomach nor guts", a person with a flat stomach will be told.

The attention given to the stomach in African sculpture is linked to its roundness, its curved lines, an expression of formal beauty. In effect, to have a well-defined stomach is not considered a disgrace in traditional African societies, it is a sign of status. The Griots or minstrels praise the belly of the chief and sing about its roundness and prominence. This roundness is part of his authority, his power of decision and his great sense of responsibility.

Children with round stomachs are highly regarded by adults because it is a sign that the mothers are feeding them well.

The legs. Their length does not matter, the only criterion is their muscularity; round or chubby legs are much sought after though bow-legs are preferred to all others.

Buttocks. Here also curved lines are preferred and developed buttocks are a sign of beauty. Women who are not particularly favoured in this area make padding for themselves which they wear beneath their clothes during big ceremonies.

In order to understand the problems which follow from the standing position when it is subjected to tension, it is necessary to understand the mechanism of the body in which the buttocks play an important role because these two muscular masses joined to the hind tilt of the pelvis furnish the structural support of the standing position. The contracted buttocks and pelvis tilted outwards produce a state of partial slump in the body.

Chapter Five
Three Levels of Teaching

In the teaching of African dance, three levels can be distinguished which correspond to the three concentric circles of African society. Dance is found all over the three circles. It conveys the spirituality of the centre towards the periphery and it is the link between the periphery and the centre in order to transcend the emotions and the aspirations.

These three levels of teaching, the glo, the caillo and the gla, correspond to dances which are taught, teachers, and pupils.

THE GLO

The Glo (village, town and by extension the crowd) translates the idea of divertissement and recreation, the expenditure of excessive energy.

Dancing in glo corresponds to the largest of the concentric circles, it encircles the village. It is the expression of relaxation and the release of tension. All the inhabitants of the village can take part if they know how to dance.

The dances in glo are solid dances. They each have a name and are characterised by precise movements and specific music. They offer dancers great possibilities of

Opposite
The drummer has a sacred and ritual quality, he is linked to the cosmic forces. Just as the Masques de Sagesse dance in the magic circles, so do the great percussionists play in the stillness of the mystic circles. The objects on the arms are thought to protect the master drummer from exhaustion and to serve as a form of inspiration.

In Africa the great percussionists, like the Grands Masques, are regarded as leaders of society. The drummers have asserted their identities through occasional risks and dangers and also their right to the vitality of their people throughout the history of black Africa. Today, these men of genius, who are more and more rare, utilise the rhythms and techniques of their people and work in a spirit of rigour. Their music is free and improvised.

A drummer from Minkengue, Republic of Congo. Height: 35.7cm. Raoul Lehuard Collection.

improvisation.[1]

Everybody, spectators and dancers, know the dance and the dancers perform it correctly. They are not here to learn to dance and thus they can transcend technique and improvise in order to achieve the joy and well-being of dancing.

Each villager standing in the centre of the dance is possessed with a fine sense of rhythm and equilibrium. They know how to coordinate their movements and also have a deep knowledge of the laws of repetition and improvisation. They master all the dances of rejoicing of their particular ethnic group because these demonstrations have been the subject of endless repetition over time.

To teach Glo raises the problem of the teacher because the dance has neither teachers nor pupils.

Glo implies that the teacher should be a dancer among others who has the sole task of training others. This teaching can be summed up as "do as I do, move as I do if you can and how you can but I am not allowed to explain it to you".

The role of the teacher is primarily to create a related climate, a group dynamic which will mean that every dancer speaks the same language. There are no pupils, properly speaking, but there are dancers trying to master the same techniques, communicating an immediate fellow-feeling during the performance of the dance, and expressing contentment and joy.

Some advice about teaching in the West

In order to teach Glo in the West it is imperative that:

— The "teacher" in charge of the dance knows several substantial dances.

— The dancers know the technique of the dances which they are performing.

— Dancers who have mastered these dances are present.

For African villagers who have been immersed in this environment since their birth, the training is easy enough if they have a sense of rhythm. On the other hand, every European should be considered a beginner in African dance and the teaching of glo is not suited to them since they do not know the dances.

Teaching glo to beginners is nonsense. Of course, although those who are more gifted at imitation can perhaps appear competent to Western eyes, the fact remains that they do not know the rules and the movements because they have not learned them. Their dances are worthless and have nothing in common with traditional African dance.

To contradict this evidence is to deny the basic technique and movement of traditional African dance. It means that imitation alone is sufficient to teach dance.

It is imperative that the "teacher", the "leader" of the dance knows more than the other dancers.

---

1 Improvisation does not mean a deformed imitation of observed gestures. There are a large number of students who have attended courses in "African dance" for between five to seven years to whom improvisation simply means trembling shoulders and head. I hope that this book will convey the information which might help them avoid such misunderstandings.

THE CAILLO 𝆕

The caillo corresponds to the second concentric circle, the intermediary between pure spirituality and the terrestrial. It is a level of teaching essential in order to achieve the following level.

The caillo (the key man, leader, responsible for collecting) is both a man of experience, who knows about human problems and the problems of the group, and a man of considerable talent. He is a master who passes on a special technique which is solid and precise.

Each dance has basic, codified, structured movements which obey strict rules dictated by tradition because of their symbolic and spiritual meaning. They are taught by the caillo.

Thus the future bearers of the mask learn to master the steps and specific gestures of the Masques de Sagesse and are taught the initiation dances.[2]

In a Kman or temple of the Masques de Sagesse, the caillo is the interpreter of the works of the great masters of the past.[3] He has a complete knowledge of the technique and the symbolism of the dances of initiation which he teaches.

Because the dances of the Elders can be applied to the letter, the course begins with technique. The caillo shows the movement to the students, explains it and performs it.

The teaching consists of analysing in several elements the basic, complex movements in order to make them more easily accessible to the students. Each of these elements can be studied separately and then the movement as a whole. If the initiating gesture is difficult for the students to reproduce, the caillo separates it and repeats the preparatory exercises until the different elements are completely assimilated.

In the caillo it is the teacher who possesses the knowledge of the movement. He alone can shape it because he knows in which ensemble the sub-movement is located. There exists a privileged relationship between the caillo and the pupils throughout the lessons and the pupils never distract attention by communicating with each other.

The caillo never reveals his final project and the pupils do not ask questions. The dance teacher is the catalyst in all the cosmic forces and he must remain the catalyst of these energies. His teaching is not limited to technique, he learns also above all to regulate the energy of each movement in order to produce the effect anticipated by the Elders.

Economy, concentration on or liberation from energy, the rise or fall of the rate

---

2 The performance of a dance which has a spiritual character does not permit any fault on the part of the dancer. Therefore any mistake during the dance of the Goumba (Mali) is thought to bring bad luck.

   In the initiation dances of the Sangnounou (west Ivory Coast) whose preparation demands years of work, any carelessness by one of the two teachers (caillo) who make three girls dance could cost the lives of the dancers since any movement which is poorly performed can harm one of the caillos.

3 Oral civilisation has always taken care to transmit faithfully the most distinguished achievements of great men to succeeding generations.

of vibration, all these depend on the type of dance which is performed. For example, the war dances performed on the field of battle require a particular training because they aim to create an esprit de corps. Each dancer must exceed his own strength in order to transmit it to "the collective" and thus to dissolve in it.

The energies necessary to invoke the blessings of the cosmos or to perform a fertility dance or to placate a madman are quite different.[4]

Some advice about teaching caillo in the West

This approach which consists of analysing a movement in sub-elements is found in jazz-ballet, in performances of contemporary dance, jazz, modern dance, and competition dances in which choreography is composed of figures working separately and then repeated in enchainments.

With regard to technique, the caillo is completely adapted to the western ethos but the caillo involves something else: the teaching of a technique in order to go beyond it. It also involves surpassing oneself and a complete knowledge of the energies on the part of the master who must remain the catalyst.

With regard to technique alone, the caillo should be the first level of teaching in the West, although the teacher should also watch the analysis of dances usually applied to glo. This allows western beginners to familiarise themselves with the dances and to acquaint themselves with the technique. Then they can follow the teaching of glo with profit and really improvise. The dance teacher should be able to distinguish between the warm-up exercises and relaxation exercises of pure dance.[5]

At a time when there is a tendency to confuse mime, dance and theatre, the rather rapid amalgamation of dance/suppleness/rhythm has spread throughout the West. Suppleness helps but is not everything since karate champions, body-building experts, gymnastic or boxing stars do not necessarily make good dancers.

To achieve this prowess with the body, to do the splits does not necessarily mean that a dancer has a sense of rhythm and the two are necessary in traditional African dance.

THE GLA ᛒ

The gla corresponds to the smallest of the concentric circles: the spiritual. Gla means

---

Opposite

Blin-doo, a dance mask from the Duekone region (western Ivory Coast), brandishes his gla koou while dancing Abla-banii, a beo dance particular to dance masks. August 1969.

According to the Elders and to tradition. Abla-banii has no meaning at all if it is performed without the gla koou (see dancing objects, p. 87).

---

4   Dance therapy is one branch of traditional African dance.
5   African languages employ different descriptions in order to distinguish between a person who is supple and a dancer.

mask and conveys an idea of immortality (man dies but the mask is eternal).

Gla exists only when the three distinct parts of which it is composed are assembled together:

— Gla blehi is the man recognised officially by the Kman as the bearer of the mask during all the ceremonies and for the rest of his life.

— Gla yiba, the face of the mask.

— Gla bledi, the features of the mask: tunic, raffia skirts, coloured baton, hat, leggings.

The kind of dances on this level of teaching are quite varied and specific. They use repetition and link technique and the control of the caillo's energies with the improvisation of the glo on a more elevated level. These are the dances of the Masques.

The gla is a level of teaching which has no justification in the West.

METHODS OF SPATIAL ARRANGEMENTS: THE TECHNIQUES

There are four dance techniques:

— *Sahan*: The dancers stand in a circle and dance in either a clockwise or an anti-clockwise direction. The dance master can be placed either in the centre of the circle, in the circle or outside the circle. It depends on what he wants to happen.

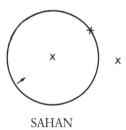

SAHAN

SAHAN
X : The possible position of the dance teacher
↗ : The direction of the glance.

—Plo:[6] The dancers stand side-by-side and dance on a line in the form of an arc. The dance teacher stands at any point along the imaginary string, or on the arc itself or even outside the geometrical figure. Everything depends on his intentions.

— *Djena*: The dancers stand side-by-side and dance in several rows.

---

6   The plo is an arc formed by a supple stem of wood or bamboo. By extension, for the Oueon, plo means any figure which describes an arc.

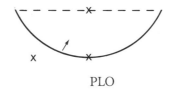

PLO   PLO

The technique of djena is a technique of practical, non-traditional instruction which corresponds to an Italian-style stage and to Western teaching. It enables both the pupils to see the teacher better and the teacher to see the pupils more easily while explaining and analysing the movements.

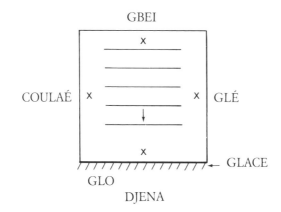

DJENA   DJENA

Names are given to the four walls of the classroom: the wall with a mirror, usually facing the students, in which everything reflected can represent the village, is called glo; the wall opposite the mirror, and thus the village, is symbolised by the encampment or gbei; the wall to the right of the students symbolised by the forest is called coula; the wall on the left symbolises the field and is calle glé.

The position of the teacher is usually in front of the dancers but he can also stand on one of the sides (coula or glé) or behind them (gbei). He can also be immersed in the group. Everything depends on the objective.

— *Sin*: the dancers are standing in Indian file and dance along a line which is either straight or curved.

Sin or snake is a technique which the great African chiefs use when they dance. Its usage assumes that the warriors have passed the stage of apprenticeship and it consists of the repetition of those basic movements essential when they are on the point of waging battle.

The dance teacher must stand at the head of the line or on one of the flanks of the column but never as part of it because it is the chief who must lead his men to the field of honour. "People never follow the finger of a wise man but his step", says one African.

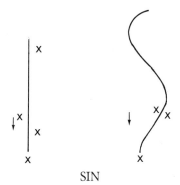

SIN   SIN

THE DIRECTIONS

In each of these techniques the dancers are arranged in four directions:

    — *Djie*: the dancers are in line with each looking at the neck of the one in front.

    — *Djiba*: The dancers face each other.

    — *Kle*: The dancers turn their backs.

    — *Gbaco*: The dancers move cheerfully to the right and left. It is worth noting that only the djena technique allows the dancers to be "gbaco in djena". (They cannot be gbaco in sahan, plo or sin).

Thus the dancers can be:

Djie in Sahan (in a circle side towards the centre).

Djiba in Sahan (in a circle looking towards the centre).

Kle in Sahan (in a circle back to the centre).

Djie in Plo (in an arc with the side towards the inside of the arc).

Djiba in Plo (in an arc looking towards the inside of the arc).

Kle in Plo (in an arc with the back turned to the inside of the arc).

Djie in Djena (facing the mirror or glo and moving towards the mirror).

Djiba in Djena (facing the mirror or glo and dancing in place).

Kle in Djena (back to the glo and moving backwards towards the glo or towards the gbei, the wall opposite the mirror).

Gbaco in Djena (the dancers move in each direction,[7] glo, gbei, coulae and gle).

Djie in Sin (a dance in Indian file moving forwards).

Djiba in Sin (a dance in place).

Kle in Sin (a dance in Indian file moving backwards).

---

7   The ambience of these dances can be seen in the meeting place of an African village.

POSITIONS

The upright position is not defined. There are three other positions:

— *Vee*: The dancers crouch.

— *Dei*: The dancers sit (the teacher should specify clearly whether the dancers are to sit with their legs stretched out or cross-legged. He should also specify whether the dancers should change position while remaining seated or whether they should get up in order to change direction).

— *Koou*: The dancers are kneeling (the teacher must indicate whether the dancers should change position while remaining on their knees).

Overleaf

A dancer, her legs in dooplé, about to execute a movement familiar to amateur and professional performers of Africa dance. This movement makes the upper limbs, chest, shoulders, shoulder-blades, vertebral column and torso work simultaneously.

Wooden statue from Makonde (Mozambique). Height: 74cm. Linden Museum, Stuttgart.

Chapter Six
Basic Movements

"When they use the word step, Europeans are making an abstract game of dance in order to raise man from the ground and to project him into the sky". Africans prefer the expression of a basic movement, dee bo in the Oueoulou language, because it emphasises the dancer's adherence to the ground and underlines the symbolic value of each dance figure.

The traditional African dancer does not attempt to escape gravity or to liberate himself from it but to come to terms with it in order to derive strength from it. He also knows that the figures he performs are not simply aesthetic but also have to be the visible expression of all the archetypal, spiritual images inscribed on the foundation of cosmic memory.

According to the dictionary, movement is a position which changes in relation to space and time, according to a system of reference.

Basic movements are the primary position of the legs which articulate every African dance.

More than the rigid positions, these are the positions or postures which change constantly. They can be multiplied infinitely and each dancer can link them according to his own inspiration, the dance and the rhythm.

These movements, ten in number, which are found in every area of Africa and amongst all its peoples are part of the African cultural heritage. Their names are taken from the initiation language of the society of the Masques de Sagesse of western Ivory Coast whose interpreters are of Oueon stock, the Guere people today, of the Krou Bete family.

They are:

— The dooplé.

— The soumplé.

— The kagnioulé.

— The kagnidjéè.

— The djiétéba.

— The doundo.

— The tchinkoui.

— The kouitchin.

— The zépiè.

— The néo.

These names, which are pure African, with no foreign root or resonance, are evidence of their origin and their age. In many African languages one can recognise "imported" or imposed words because they retain a foreign resonance. This practice, which is useful in the study of ethnography, distinguishes immediately between what is part of indigenous culture and what has been imported from foreign culture.[1]

Each of the basic movements is didactic and conceals a teaching which is both physical and spiritual[2] just like their names which also have a double meaning.

DOOPLÉ

Dooplé consists of two words: doo, concrete or mortar, and plé, the need to run. The literal translation of dooplé is a mortar run or race and, by extension, vibrating, jumping, stirring, flying, starting, a concrete dance.

For the Masques de Sagesse, the mortar, because of its robustness, its equilibrium, its solidity and its adherence to the ground, is the symbol of the human being standing "feet on the ground" in the middle of a world and linked to the work of creation.[3]

Doo is the mother with her welcoming attitude, noble, the image of maturity in life, according to African tradition the first living being on earth.[4]

Because it is both hollow and a container, the mortar is also the symbol of the mother, the primary element, static, restful and welcoming who awaits the active, dynamic element.

The first basic movement is thus the mother-position which constitutes the very

---

1   Many African languages use a linguistic association of ideas. In Oueoulou ban means far or distant. Ban-on means traders "those who come from far away": the people of Bambara, Dioula and Malinke who live in northern Ivory Coast, a considerable distance from western Ivory Coast.

　　The horse (soo in Bambara) is called Ban-Soo in Oueoulou and means a breed of horse which comes from far away. Thus it appears that the Oueon had never seen a horse until the arrival of the traders from Malinke, Bambara and Dioula in their region.

　　Ninguin-soo (iron horse) or Toubabou-soo (white horse) in familiar language means bicycle in Bambara. This precision distinguishes the animal from the object and is an indication of its provenance and from this it is obvious that the bicycle was not invented by the blacksmiths of Bambara.

　　In the same way becani (bicycle in Oueoulou) refers to the people who first made it known to the Oueon.

2   See the beo and gnenon dances, p. 29.

3   This conforms with the Masques de Sagesse who teach that in order to achieve the fulfilment and development of man, the spiritual and the physical are two aspects of the same reality and not separate and conflicting worlds.

4   This idea of passive solidity while waiting is linked to African matriarchy. There are many African stories and riddles which preserve the memory of woman as the first being seen on earth (man only came later). There are also many societies whose genealogies are still based on a matriarchal line, as in more primitive periods.

nucleus around which the other nine basic movements gravitate.

Doo, the mortar, occupies a select place in African village life. It is an indispens-able part of daily life in order to pound the food and prepare remedies. The word is used in numerous expressions.[5]

It is living evidence just like the details of a tree trunk and it is part of the rejuvenation of vital growth and, like all wood, it is charged with a special energy.

It is also the natural foundation for certain invocations,[6] and the sounds of a mortar when it is being pounded by a pestle are part of the preparation of remedies for mentally ill people.

Doo is also called the first in Oueoulou, the ordinal, numeral adjective which indicates the rank of the movement in the category of African dance figures.

Plé in dooplé is the life which governs rest, rest whose primary peculiarity is to be constantly in motion.

Plé represents the heart of the mother who dances with joy at the sight of her child. It is the divine spark.

In the language of the Masques it is also the symbol of the unique force which detaches the leaf from the tree and which directs the migrating birds over thousands of miles. It also makes children smile and governs the course of the sun and directs one's own talents.

Plé is the life in matter which is apparently inert but constantly in movement, it is the incessant dance of particles throughout the universe.

Plé is a reminder that this activity constitutes the profound essence of the Being and that dance is a manifestation of life.

The dooplé is undoubtedly, the most natural, the most authentic and the oldest basic movement in African dance.[7] It is both the melting pot and the locomotive of African dance through which the dancer's personality is annihilated in order to be recreated in a new form.

Drawings, paintings, photographs and sculptures are evidence of the knowledge of dooplé throughout all of black Africa and it is found in thousands of dances: Zulu war dances, the mystical and aerial dances of the Guere, the magical dances of the Hausa (Niger), the acrobatic dances of Guinea, Mali, Burkina Fasso, the sensual dances of the Congo, Cameroon and Zaire, individual or collective dances (the "low dances" performed terre-a-terre) or "upward dances" (jumped dances).

---

5   Breakfast and lunch are called "morning mortar"; dinner is "evening mortar". A "family without mortar" is a family condemned to famine and wretchedness. A person "without mortar" cannot earn a living.

6   They are used in baptismal ceremonies which existed in Africa before the arrival of official religions.

7   The frescoes and small figures of the Sahara show this attitude. "According to neolithic evidence men and women, without discrimination or specification, both had this dance pose—bent legs, hands held above—the early mixed dance scene at Jabbaren-Amazzar is clear proof of this...". J. Bernolles, *Permanence de la parure et du masque africain*.

    "The legs are treated coarsely and have a characteristically ritual position in all upright statuettes. They are clearly bent at the knee...The Teke visualise the human body as being composed of three parts: the head..., the trunk...and the legs which are always bent as in the dance of the men (Nkibi)..."

    Extracts from a work by Robert Hottot written during two expeditions to the region of Teke (Congo) in 1906 and referred to during a conference in 1933.

All the dancers are in dooplé, except the man with his back to the camera in the foreground who is in kouitchin. The young girl (third from the left) has her feet in dooplé and her thighs in soumplé. Her arms are in gba, like those of the man in front of her.

An atchangbekon dance from Tabligbo, Togo. September 1963.

When studying the techniques of certain specific basic principles in African dance, there are some essential features to be noted, especially the pounding of the ground by the heel, the external side of the arch of the foot, the underside of the toes and by demi-pointe and the sole of the foot.

It is through dooplé that Africans are past masters in the art of vibrating the shoulders, the chest and the head while beating the ground with their feet.

It is the same dooplé which has made them the greatest exponents of swaying hips and pelvic movements.

Dooplé is present inexorably at the very heart of contemporary African creativity, despite the wish by some people to purify authentic African gestures.[8]

The other basic movements are all the products of dooplé which remains the necessary springboard for the exploitation and creation of new gestures to symbolise the sea, love, life or ideas.

Description of the dancer in dooplé

The dancer is standing, his knees are bent and the thighs are not held close together.

His feet, placed parallel and flat, keep close to the ground and are wide apart by between thirty to forty centimetres according to the length of the dancer's feet.

The torso, bent slightly forwards, forms with the pelvis an angle of about 135 degrees.

There is no contraction or rigidity about the buttocks or the pelvis. The arms are either pressed against the body or carried slightly in front or clearly raised above.

The hands remain open, in plo, or are closed.

The gaze is fixed on the horizon.

In this position the African dancer is a participant, he finds himself and concentrates, he lives with gravity and draws to himself all the surrounding energies in order to sustain him. He is at one with the earth-mother and the whole world.

This position, which is peculiar to African dance, is very aesthetic and does not require any superfluous contractions; on the contrary it produces an extraordinary quality of relaxation[9] which is a guarantee of the dancer's symbiotic state with his environment. Thus the great traditional dancers, despite the speed of their movements, keep parts of the legs relaxed and flowing, almost lazy. The legs which are bent permanently allow the dancer to shape his "jumps" the way he wants and to rise up and grow taller during certain moments of the dance.

The arms and head are balanced without rigidity, with the result that the body is swept by multiple waves which focus the energy of the movement at the points where the waves intersect: the shoulders, the pelvis and the vertebral column.

The origin of the dooplé

Jacques Bernolles, one of the few researchers to be interested in the basic movement of the dooplé, has questioned the origin of the dooplé. He hypothesises that it was the Pygmies who created the dooplé and that it was the sight of monkeys dancing erect which could have given the Pygmies the idea of this movement.

It seems to me that the consecration of the dooplé was even more simple. This position of bent knees is the most natural human pose (it is the baby's foetal position), the most stable (it is how the baby learns to walk), the most balanced, the most bracing, the most economic in its energy (for example, the racing cyclist uses it and it also enables the dancer to work without interruption from between six to

---

8   "La Solitude d'Être", by Elsa Wolliaston, Arles Festival, July 1988.
9   "This physical posture allows the pressure to be transmitted to the knees which have the role of shock-absorbers...the flexibility of the knee is fundamental to the efficient working of the lower body...The walk backwards gains in power if the knees are bent. It becomes dangerous if they are not bent and can lead to serious injuries". Doctor Alexandre Lowen.

eight hours). It is also the most effective in "recovery".[10] Is it not the one most often used by runners after they have cleared the finishing line?

Some see dooplé as a symbol. Bernolles suggests a game of love, a fertility dance, a cosmogonic dance connecting the dooplé to ancient Greek representations. But he stresses that these are only hypotheses.

The African is the opposite of the Greek artist who was inspired by the individual and by human figures in order to articulate the divine. He begins with his experience of the cosmos in order to give a concrete form to his work. The African has a global vision and for him body and soul, art and religion are one.

For him dance is a complete language, a means of communication with himself, with others and with eternity.

Once again in this dance there are the three concentric circles. Dooplé, the most natural human position (the largest circle and the most human), also the mother of all basic movements (the smallest circle, the most "spiritual") is the indispensable element in the transition from one circle to another, from one level to another.

THE SOUMPLÉ

Soumplé or somplé, the second basic movement, means literally the course of the pestle.

Plé: course, hollow, dance, symbolising the visible or invisible force, the propulsive energy. Soum, the pestle, in African manners and customs, is the companion of the mortar which it completes.

This complementarity is emphasised in the language by the fact that doo and soum are fairly rare twin names.[11]

The pestle is both useful and essential to the mortar. It grinds the contents of the mortar and is thus the dynamic element which encounters the passive element. The route of the pestle in the mortar gives birth to another fundamental element in the sun dance: rhythm.

The dance of the pestle in the mortar is sustained by percussion according to the rhythm produced by their communion.

Soumplé is an ordinal numeral adjective indicating its place in the scale of basic movements. As the second movement, it symbolises man and comes after woman. Dooplé and soumplé represent opposites through which realities engendered in the

---

10 One of the first injunctions in bio-energy therapy is an exact repetition of an order in traditional African dance: "Keep the knees bent".

"To hold the knees straight creates an illusion of security...if the legs are flexible and relaxed, the pressure which comes from above is transmitted to the legs and is discharged into the ground..." writes Doctor Alexander Lowen, the father of bio-energy and leader of this new school of American practitioners who try to give their patients access to the full exercise of physical and psychical life.

11 Among the Oueon, twins are called Gba gnounou, children who balance and complement each other. Zirignounou refers to children who have powers which are inexplicable or incomprehensible (clairvoyance, healing powers). For certain peoples, such as the Mossi, twins are beings from another world whom they fear.

A young dancer in soumplé; her knees are bent, her feet are together.

Pounou statuette, Gabon. Height: 30cm. Private collection.

universe complement each other. They need each other in order to get the best from each other.

The soumplé position

As in the dooplé, the knees are bent and the feet are placed flat and parallel, firmly on the ground.

But in the soumplé the feet, legs and thighs are close together. Soumplé allows the body of the dancer to function during the dance as an accumulator or dispenser of energy.

THE KAGNIOULÉ

The two primary basic movements, masculine and feminine principles being represented by the mortar and pestle, symbolise the two opposing principles of life which are found in Chinese culture with yin and yang and produce the third basic movement, the kagnioulé, symbol of the first man/god.

According to the story of the Masques, Kagni is the name of the first dance mask to appear on earth. Half-god (mask), half-man (the wearer of the mask), he was sent by the Mother of Masks in order to teach dance to men but his role was also that of intermediary between men and the double entity of the On-High.

Oulé comes from Ouloa, the new-born. Among the Guere, to say that a Mask is about to be born is to say that it is about to dance. Thus Ouloa means to be born and to dance.

Oulé is the name of a dance which is frequently performed in western Ivory Coast.

During the performance of the dance the Kagni mask makes man sensitive to a philosophy common throughout Africa: "He who knows must always give an example" and also " In order to teach dance one must be a dancer oneself".

The kagnioulé position

As in the dooplé, in the basic kagnioulé movement the knees are bent; the feet are placed flat and parallel, firmly on the ground. The length of the dancer's foot, about 35 to 40 centimetres, should separate them. The legs and thighs should be close together. But the body weight should be transferred on one foot only. The foot of the leg which is not supporting the body is placed on half-point on the ground, at the same level as the arch of the sole of the other foot. This position in demi-point leads to an accentuation of the flexing of the knee.

The foot of the supporting leg remains firmly on the ground.

The knee of this leg fits into the hollow formed by the flexing of the other knee.

The two legs form a compact and this gives them a homogenous image.

The legs of the dancer are in kagnioulé. In the mirror his left arm appears to be in ploa gbaou but in reality it is in gba at elbow level.

The right arm is in naou.

The torso and the head are in sahan and not in ploa gbaou, as the reflection in the mirror would imply.

In the mirror the right hand seems to be in djerin but it is, in fact, in bloagnon.

The other gba consist of the angle formed by the raised right arm and the back (profile and front) and the angle formed in the mirror by the torso and the leg.

The angle formed by the feet and the legs are also gba.

THE DOOPLÉ, THE KAGNIOULÉ AND SLAVERY

One of the most significant dances from the point of the combination of dooplé and kagnioulé is the one which recalls slavery which is performed in various ways throughout the whole of Africa.

Every race at some moment in its history has been confronted with the problem of slavery. There are various motifs which man has employed in order to deprive his fellow creatures of their freedom and to regard them as mere merchandise. There were social rules such as birth, marriage, conviction for debt, religious intolerance, also war and its attendant prisoners and deportees, loot, treasure obtained by war, piracy and abduction.

Western statuary, in which slaves are often represented, provides evidence of this long history.[12]

In Africa also enslavement, domination and oppression have been a source of profound inspiration for artists.

The percussion players know how to make the drums speak, stirring up new energies and forces. They have given percussion its rightful place in contemporary musical creation.

The Griots or minstrels, in the face of oppression, have sung about the close bonds which link man to the universe, to the cosmos and to God. The masterpieces which they created have become classic African stories.

The slaves in the cotton fields invented jazz, dance music which compels the body to move, "language, communion, the complete expression of existence from every community to each generation", to which geniuses like Louis Armstrong, Count Basie, Dizzy Gillespie and so many others have made such a noble contribution.

African sculptors have also provided evidence of this exploitation but of all the African arts it is dance which has been the best illustration of slavery.

Slave Dance

At the beginning of the dance the dancer, clad in a loincloth, legs in kagnioulé, stands in the middle of a huge dance-floor which represents a village meeting-place. Around him a crowd forms a circumference of between five to seven centimetres.

The dancer's head is inclined slightly towards the ground and his eyes are fixed on the ground. Seen in profile, the torso bent forwards forms with the pelvis an angle of 135 degrees. From the leg which supports the body weight (foot flat on the ground) to the top of the head, the body forms a half-moon or half-circle sustained by a string which connects the big toe to the middle of the dancer's front.

From the back, the arms of the dancer seem linked to the wrists. The palms of the hands are open and turned towards the sky.

The line connecting the shoulders and the arms create a triangle whose angle formed by the wrists is bisected by the vertebral column. This produces two triangles on the dancer's body.

From the front the face of the dancer is made up. The body is painted with a mixture of roots, leaves and earth crushed together in a mortar.

Suddenly the drum master begins a dialogue with nature through sounds which are powerful, heavy, muffled, menacing, uneasy.

Subdued, possessed by these sonorities which tell of the direct connections between all people who suffer, the crowd remains mute, disconcerted, paralysed, their attention captured by the extraordinary presence of the dancer who has not moved.

---

12 Some examples are the Ethiopian slave of Chalon-sur Saone, the Barbary prisoners in the Louvre, the heads and busts of the slaves in Trajan's time, the well-known slaves on the tomb of Julius II sculpted by Michelangelo, and the slaves in the Salon de la Guerre or in the gardens at Versailles.

After a series of improvisations the drum master pauses. The dancer, freed from his uneasiness, throws back his shoulders as if, exhausted, he was seeking to stretch his shoulders. The drum begins again this time with the specific rhythm of the "slave dance".

In rhythm, with the head always unmoving, the dancer moves from the simple throwing back of the shoulders to more complex movements in which the shoulders are now connected to undulating movements of the torso.

In the throwing back of the shoulders the birth of the movement is located at the level of the shoulder-blades. On the back, the undulations begin at the level of the solar plexus, a gesture which is very difficult to master.

Analysis of the movement

I—The chest swells, the back hollows. The movement is dry and brief; it is transmitted through the shoulders which remain solid. From the back the wrists do not change place.

II—The chest is drawn in, the back becomes slightly round, it is drawn up slightly in order to regain its initial position.

During the dance the second is equivalent to AND, in half-time.

Until now the dancer has not changed his place either to the front or the back. His dance was restricted to the torso, the back, the stomach, the arms and the shoulders. There is no expression at all in the hands or the arms which stick closely to the back and to the body. The head remains immobile, the eyes are fixed on the ground.

From time to time, in harmony with the percussion, the dancer stops his undulating movements in order to make his whole body quiver. The vibrations follow the lines of the legs, the torso and the head.

The drummer utters a cry and immediately changes the variation. At once, at regular intervals, the dancer jumps, in front, behind or to the side, in conformity with a very precise technique. He moves his feet with method and skill.

He changes feet on the third AND, that is when the chest expands.

He places the foot in the kagnioulé position (foot flat on the ground, the other foot on half-point.

Each shift in weight always begins with the foot on half-point, whatever the direction of the shift:

(a) the dancer completely detaches the foot on half-point from the ground, the point directed downwards.

(b) the foot, still on half-point and not on the sole of the foot, is put on the ground in place of the other foot.

The rest of the sole of the foot only touches the ground on a second beat when, simultaneously, the foot on which the body weight rests at the start of a jump holds itself in demi-point at the level of its internal impulse.

Thus there is a transfer of the body weight from one leg to another at the end of each jump or step. The evolution is achieved thus:

ONE (the undulation of the torso) AND (the chest expands) TWO (undulation of the torso) AND (the chest expands) THREE (undulation of the torso) AND (the beat of the walk or the jump during which the body weight is transferred from one leg to the other).

The drummer marks a stop and encompasses almost immediately a world of different rhythms which animate the crowd. Contrary to the anguished and sad language of the first part of the dance, the sounds are lively, cheerful, joyful. Faces are relaxed, the audience begins to enjoy itself again.

The initiative of the drummer transforms the dancer. Becoming free and liberated himself, he also makes the rhythm more free. For the first time his head straightens up. His gaze leaves the ground in order to embrace life. His feet, free of chains "chatter and quarrel together like doves". His back twists itself into curves, circles and spirals. His arms evoke the wings of a bird, the waves or the branches of a palm tree. Possessed by the fire of life and liberty, he "dances" his walk, his direction, his jumps, he dances his life.

The audience, moved, observes the harmonious coordination and extraordinary beauty of these singular gestures through which the dancer relates with skill and grace the most touching and dramatic story in human history.

THE KAGNIDJÉÈ

Kagni is the root of the verb "kagnindi" to open. It is also the mask Kagni, the first Mask of the Dance.

Djié is the abbreviation of Djiekpourou, the way, the path, the route, the track.

Kagnidjéè thus means that the Kagni mask opens the way of the dance and poses as the first performer of this art with the desire to enlarge human relations and to repel solitude, indifference, the lack of communication.

Kagni opens the way of dance with the dance becoming the dancer himself.

There is no gulf between the essence and the appearance and this basic movement is a good illustration of the African imagination, according to which teaching is taught by example and not by intellectual speculations and should also be the result of experience: "humanity never follows the finger of the wise man only his step", "never teach others what your own soul can better experience".

Kagnidjéè leads to respect for the body and reveals it to be the most prodigious of instruments, the most fantastic of machines. Everyone should know the body better in order to get the best from it.

In the kagnidjéè movement:

The knees are bent and the feet are flat, firmly on the ground, separated by a space the size of the dancer's foot, as in the dooplé;

— The thighs are crossed but close together at the level of the knees;

— The legs, separated by a space, are crossed from the knees down;

— The foot of the crossing leg is placed on the ground in front of the other and touches the ground with the sole of the foot, either on half-point or by the heel;

— The knee of the hind leg fits lightly into the knee of the crossing leg;

— The foot of the hind leg is placed flat or on half-point; its point is vertical to the outside edge the front foot.

This position recalls a position in Asian dances.

The gestures of kagnidjéè project and are non-descriptive. It opens up a world which cannot be translated by words.

The fourth basic movement is in one sense the second of the three concentric circles. Its dance is complete, independent, indescribable but its message is perceived because Kagni opens the way and is the intermediary between the universe and man.

THE DJIÉTÉBA

The fifth basic movement, djiétéba, (from djie, a path, and teba, to conduct or to lead) is an invitation to dance: come, dance on the path, on the dance-floor.

Kagni invites everyone to take part in the dance on the floor, in the centre of the village. Everyone must accompany the dance and help it to proceed.

djiétéba depends completely on dooplé and from it comes its strength, suppleness, fluidity and personality.

From dooplé it keeps the knees bent, the feet placed flat, close to the ground and separated from each other by a space the length of the dancer's foot.

Dooplé is changed into djiétéba when:

One leg carries all the body weight and the knee remains bent;

The other leg extends to the side at a distance equal to the length of the dancer's foot, the heel placed at right angles to the foot of the bent leg;

The position recalls the legs of Cossack dancers but is less bent.

The exploration of djiétéba has given birth to many rhythmic dances, such as the "forward danced walk" which puts the accent on the undulation of the torso from top to bottom and whose impulses separate the heels, knees and pelvis.

The djiétéba exercises make the hips more flexible and release the pelvis. In learning to be one with the dance and percussion, the djiétéba can lead to a harmonious and graceful shifting of weight.

This "danced forward walk", associated with many expressions of the hands and arms, helps me to focus these exercises in order to explain to my pupils that, for the Africans, any body which does not have complete and harmonious circulation of energy is a handicapped body, and will never know the fundamental peace which pure dance brings and which is essential in order to perform "divine" dances.

THE DOUNDO

The sixth basic movement is certainly one of the most difficult to perform.

In the doundo (from doun, snail shells, and do, percussion beat) the dancer is in the last spiral, the third concentric circle, the most spiritual, and he tries somehow to fix himself and remain there for as long as possible but he cannot remain there long.

It is a transitional state, an intrusion into another world in which the whole body is saturated with everything he finds there in order to retranslate it into all his actions.

The movement expresses this attempt: the dancer stands balanced on his heels which must be parallel but separated by the length of the dancer's foot. As in the dooplé, the starting point is bent knees and feet placed flat separated by a distance of thirty to forty centimetres.

This movement involves a rapid percussion rhythm and causes considerable excitement.

THE TCHINKOUI

The seventh basic movement celebrates all the movements of absence and presence, of the yes and the no.

As its name indicates (tchin, to slice, and koui, body), the tchinkoui expresses the attempt to sublimate the body, to purify the body chained to the earth, to separate it.

The position is like that of the doopié:

Bent knees;

Feet separated by the length of the dancer's foot;

All the body weight is supported by the right leg which rests only on the outside edge of the foot;

The inside edge of the left foot rests with great suppleness on the ground;

The right hip is directed outwards.

Overleaf

Feet in kouitchin. Note the length of the neck and the rounded shapes of the shoulders and arms.

Sculpture of a pregnant Bamileke woman, Cameroon. Height: 161cm. Staatliches Museum for Volker-kunde, Munich.

THE KOUITCHIN

In kouitchin there are the same features as in tchinkoui but in reverse order: kou, body, koui the soul and tchin: to cut.

In the preceding movement the body tried to refine itself in order to fuse with the soul. In this movement the body interrupts, stops, makes the dancer go down or rise above the ground.

The position of the feet expresses this return to the ground because the kouitchin is characterised by turned-in feet.[13] At the level of the legs and the feet this determines two triangles whose common base is the line which connects the two heels and whose apexes are, respectively, the junction point of the knees and the contact point of the big toes.

The knees are bent and the thighs remain close together as in the dooplé;
The two big toes touch each other;
The heels turn out and are separated by the length of the dancer's foot;
The bent knees touch other;
The legs are separated.

The apex of the triangle formed by the flat feet indicates the direction on the horizon the dancer's nose must take.

THE ZÉPIÉ

The word consists of ze, to balance, and péé, the fibre of the palm-tree, symbol of the link between God and man.

In this basic movement, the dancer is balanced like a palm leaf. The position is practically identical to that of the dooplé, with the exception of the feet which, instead of being placed flat on the ground, are on half-point, with the knees bent. The zépié position can be taken with feet turned in, out, or in parallel.[14]

The half-points of the zépié are a symbol of the nostalgia of the dancer who is obliged to descend to the world of the body and remove himself from the world of the pure soul. It is a return to the largest circle, to the full awareness of the body.

THE NEO

This is a state of clay, the position from which man comes and to which he will return, his usual position when he does not dance. It is man bound to the earth. This is the normal position of upright man when he is not ready to dance: upright, straight, arms dangling.

---

13 This position—knees slightly bent and feet turned in forming a triangle—is adopted instinctively by those who have to stand and listen to long official speeches because it is the most stable.

14 Turned-in feet conforms to formal African ideas of beauty. The legs are bow-shaped and refer once again to the curved lines of African dance.

This state symbolises the materiality of man, his physical surroundings. He is one of the creatures of the earth.

The therapeutic virtues of kaolin and white clay are well-known but kaolin is particularly regarded by Africans as a symbol of contentment and joy.

Contentment is the harvest which means the end of the constraints of hunger. At the end of every day during the rice harvest the young girls paint their bodies with kaolin.

It is the main make-up used by the Masques de Sagesse and the Elders paint the whole body with kaolin during ceremonies of investiture.

During the dance the presence of kaolin on the bodies of the dancers is both a symbol of contentment and a reminder that the dancer is similar to clay, that he is ready to be modelled. Regarding the creation of new gestures—which are dictated to him by his own internal being—and the progress of his thoughts, man becomes what he thinks deep within himself or what he wishes.

It is said that an African dancer is in a clayey state when he is in the neo position. He is ready to attempt movements which inspire him or which are inspired by him.

Opposite

African statuary, which has been described as "living immobility", gives material form to the basic movements of African dance and emphasis the nudity of the dancers. This reminds us of the importance of nudity and its different meaning in African culture.

A pole-statue from Metoko, Zaire. The legs are in dooplé, the feet in kouitchin. Height: 108cm. Georges-Jacques Haefeli Collection.

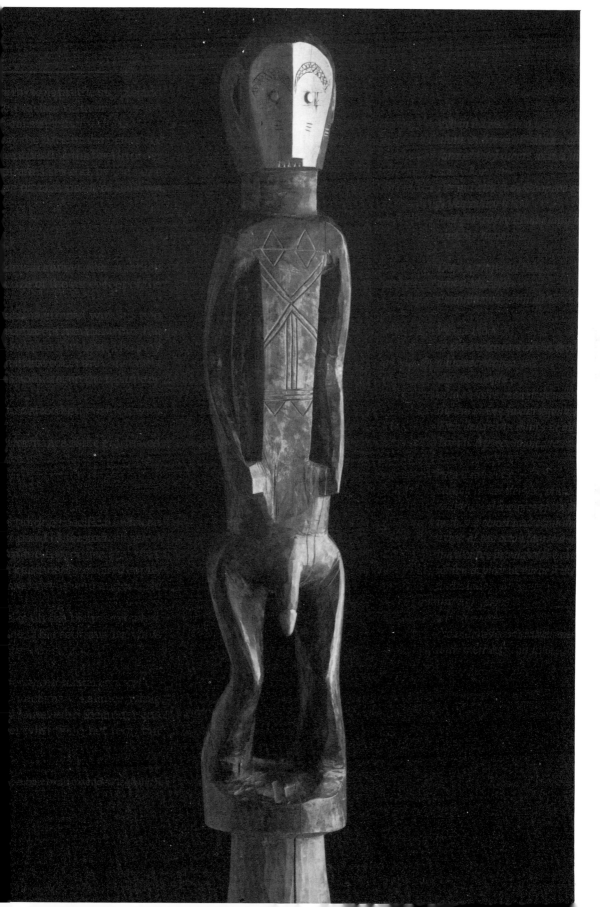

Chapter Seven
The Basic Techniques

THE POSITIONS OF THE FEET

The way to place the feet on the ground is an important element in the technique of African dance. The various possibilities depend largely on the dance which is being performed.

The placement of the foot flat on the ground

This technique, as old as the world, is one of the most difficult to master because it looks so simple.

The art of dance lies in the manner in which the foot is placed flat on the ground and in which the body is given the necessary impulsion in order to obtain a precise movement.

In certain dances, such as the Agbaza of the Ewe (Togo), the way the dancer places his foot on the ground enables him to make the whole body vibrate. This technique produces a play of the legs which is regular, restrained and aesthetic.

Pounding the ground with the heel

The great secret of the art of shifting weight lies in the way the heel beats the ground.

The act of beating the ground with the heel emphasises the buttocks corresponding to the stretched leg. Two possibilities are offered to the dancer to draw in the buttocks:

— Simply contract the buttocks without the intervention of the extended leg;

— Bring the leg and the foot back to the level of the ankle of the other leg on which rests the entire body weight in the kagnioulé position.

This operation, which must be achieved with suppleness and without rigidity, produces an oscillating movement of the leg and the buttocks which affects the whole pelvis and leads to a shift of weight which can be exciting to watch.

The beauty and the strength of this shifting weight are amplified when both legs are used and this sets the whole torso in motion.

This technique is a constant invitation to be aware that "everything stiff is lifeless" in traditional African dance. This is the golden rule which explains the supple and relaxed comportment of African dance masters in the practice of their art, even when certain movements (acrobatic jumps, amplitude) constrict their efforts.

Movements in which the neck, the shoulders, the torso, the back or the pelvis are stiff and rigid or retracted can benefit from this technique of beating the heel in order to acquire or rediscover the suppleness and agility of their muscles and, by the same token, to revitalise the whole body because to be aware of each point of his own body is to return life to it.

Pounding the ground with the outside edge of the foot

Beating the ground with the outside edge of the foot is almost always accompanied by a simultaneous beating of the ground by the inside edge of the other foot of the dancer.

The dancer begins to dance by simultaneously beating the ground with his two feet. This technique allows the dancer to use the legs in a different manner from that of hammering the legs and it increases the beauty of the shifting weight. The play of the legs is more fluid, but also more sustained because the two feet are constantly in a kagnioulé position and are never removed from the ground as in the technique of hammering.

In this technique the knees go from a flexed position to a stretched position with each shift of weight by the dancer.

This beat by the edge of the foot which is used in the performance of the graduated step of the goumbé is widespread throughout west Africa.

Pounding the ground with the underside of the toes

Beating the ground with the underside of the toes is a technique specific to African dance which has nothing in common with the stretched point of western classical dance[1] and which western performers have found difficult to reproduce.

In order to achieve this beating of the ground, the dancer must begin in dooplé, then make the body weight sway on one of the legs whose knee is bent and whose foot is placed flat on the ground.

The foot of the other leg (it is also bent at the knee) rests on the big toe which is pointing towards the ground: the dancer is in kagnioulé. This foot must always remain parallel with the other at a distance of seven centimetres.

The torso or the bust must be slightly bent forward.

The arms are placed in the position like that of a runner about to start a race.

The dancer raises the foot gently in kagnioulé which acts as a balance while remaining bent and begins to beat or rather to caress the ground with the underside of his toes. The toes touch the ground on a line parallel with the other foot, but approximately ten centimetres in front of it.

---

1   In western dance the concern for a straight leg means that the point is part of an extended leg which is stretched and stiff.

The action is carried out obliquely from top to bottom; it is gradually intensified and accelerated until the speed required for the chosen dance is achieved.

When this speed is reached the dancer must stiffen, tighten and contract the toes every time they touch the ground and then immediately release them when they leave the ground.

Thus the toes are relaxed during their trajectory in space and contracted for the whole time they are in contact with the ground.

The beauty of the play of the legs and the charm of the style depends on this alternation of contraction and release. To sustain it throughout the dance demands a virtuoso talent.

Beating the ground in this way enables the dancer to perform higher and higher acrobatic jumps, as if he were thrown up by springs every time he touches the ground.

In playing the role of shock-absorbers during each jump, the toes slacken the foot and soften the fall on the heel.

This technique means that African dancers can perform for many hours without any strain on the ankles, cramps in the calves, swollen legs or back problems.

Points

Although Africans knew about points, they did not use them in their original dances.

The use of points came about during the Romantic movement of the nineteenth century and gave the impression that the Western classical ballerina was playing with gravity. The rules concerning port de bras, balance, equilibrium, epaulement, ballon, attitude, arabesque and enchainments were codified by Carlo Blasis,[2]

dancer, choreographer, and theoretician of Italian dance who taught some of the great international dancers of the time.

The ballerina Genevieve Gosselin had used points regularly from 1813 onwards, as did Amelia Brugnoli, a pupil of Coulon, and the Russian dancer Istomina in the same period. But it was Marie Taglioni who became the embodiment of the technique later in 1831.[3]

Gestures of the head and hands

As in all genres of dances, the positions of the head and the hands are of primary importance.

Some of them are observed directly from nature, such as the Nai position (arms extended and hands hanging down without any contraction) probably inspired by the wings of large birds whose beauty and nobility have always fascinated human

---

2 Carlo Blasis, *Traite élémentaire, Theorie et pratique de la danse*, Milan 1820. In 1830 he published his *Code of Terpsichore* in London, a complete manual of dance, and the basis of most dance teaching for many years.
3 See Paul Bourcier, *Histoire de la danse en Occident*.

vision and imagination.

The Tiro is a dance gesture which consists of stretching the neck, agitating and making the head spin. It is a gesture which tries to reproduce the length, the beauty and the suppleness of guinea-fowl, giraffes and gazelles.

With this gesture African dancers achieve three aims:

— The separation of the neck from the shoulders: the extension of the neck outwards is a formal criterion of beauty in Africa, Nefertiti being a particular example.

— The stimulation and relaxation of the brain making a hollow in the head and using a lot of energy.

— The achievement of a semi-conscious state with these exercises and with the help of percussion.

Goué

This characteristic movement of the chimpanzee was taught by hunters. Many African stories mention that these great monkeys had considerable influence on the way that humans danced.

The story of Gbecon, a traditional African dance, performed by the Ewe of Togo, is one illustration of this:

"One day a hunter who was pursuing some game penetrated the heart of the forest. Suddenly he heard a wild rhythm which electrified him, drew him on and made him forget his quarry. Guided by the music he arrived at the edge of a glade. There, to his great surprise, he discovered chimpanzees performing a dance which was unknown to him, to the palpitating rhythm of an orchestra.

The hunter listened attentively to the music, watched the dancers discreetly and then returned to his village. Some days later, the Gbecon dance was born".

Sondohou

Certain African peoples symbolise life through the sondohou, a rounded, spiral snail shell, or a spiral or ellipsoid figure which have been found on the walls of round huts and which today have an honoured place in the educational games of young village people.

The gesture symbolises the concept of reincarnation.

Gaéè

This gesture, which is both a sign and an invitation to Gohin or the dance of the mad, is forbidden outside this dance.

The arm is extended and the hand does not form any angle with it. The hand is mainly open, with the palm facing the audience, the fingers are separated and

stretched.

Through this gesture the Africans mix the sacred and the profane, the solemn and the comic. They parody the serious and make fun of what they adore.

In the gaéè (unfolding), the man aspires to freedom, to realisation. He wants to conquer the moment in which everything will be allowed to him.

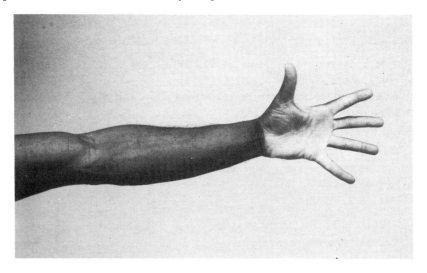

The Gohin is a game which refers to this eternal aspiration, never satisfied, for equality. It is a dance releasing tensions which represents an ideal society in which class distinctions are abolished, a world in which those who are paupers, materially and spiritually, become the lords. In this joyful dance, the gaéè expresses this old aspiration as the world in which "the last shall be first".

For several hours it gives everybody, whatever their origin and social status, an imaginary sense of power. During the dance everybody is equal and is allowed to say openly whatever goes through their heads. Men and women use a coarse vocabulary which is usually forbidden. They describe scenes of copulation or openly criticise their superiors.

Coula

When the face, the front, the front part of a limb, a part of the body, or the whole body is placed flat on the ground, it is said that the part or the body is in coula.

Thus a hand whose palm is flat on the ground is in coula. The fingers are close together.

In the same way, a dancer lying on his stomach with his face against the ground, is in coula.

Gbé

When the back, the behind, the hind part of a limb, of the body or of the whole body is flat on the ground, then it is in gbé.

Thus a dancer whose palm is turned towards the sky and who is lying on his back is in gbé. The fingers are close together.

A dancer on his back with the nape on his neck on the ground is in gbé.

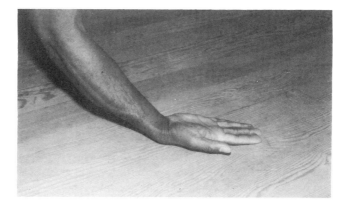

Djerin

The arm and the hand are in the same position as gbé but they are turned back with the thumb held close.

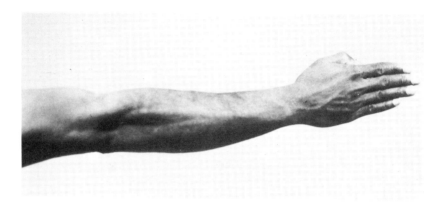

Bloa

This gesture indicates the direction of the ground. The palm of the hand is in bloa when it is turned towards the ground but there is no contact with the ground.

The arm is extended and the hand forms with it an angle of approximately ninety degrees. The fingers are close together.

Bloagnan

This indicates the horizontal line which concerns the eyes, the face, a limb or the body.

The gaze of a dancer is in bloagnan when he stares at the horizon.

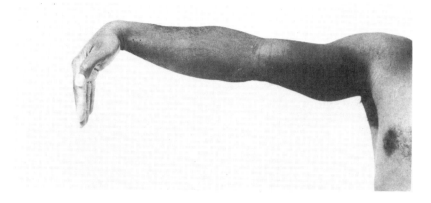

A hand extended in djerin with the palm in bloagnan.

The arm is extended. The hand is placed so that it forms an almost right angle with the arm at wrist level. The fingers are close together.

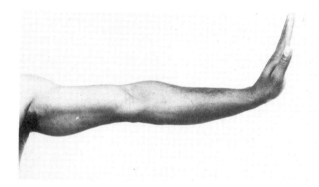

Bloade

This also indicates the horizontal line but is the opposite to bloagnan. Thus the hand extended in djerin has its back in bloade.

The nape of the dancer standing upright is in bloade, and in general if the back, hind part of a limb, or the whole body traces a horizontal line it is in bloade.

Plo

The arm is extended and the hand does not form an angle with it. An angle of more than 90 degrees is formed by the fold of the hand at the level of the fingers which are close together. The palm is not completely turned upwards.

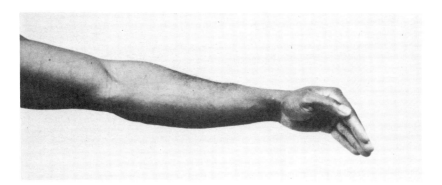

Koua

The arm is extended. The palm of the hand is turned towards the spectators. The fingers are closed, the thumb is on the outside.

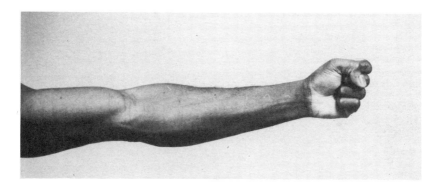

Djaon

This gesture indicates the direction of the sky. The palm of the hand is in djaon when it is turned upwards and when the back of the hand is not in contact with the ground.

The dancer, an intermediary between the sky and the earth, symbolically welcomes the sky when his hands are in djaon. By contrast he gives back what he has received when his hands are in bloa.

Overleaf

This dancer, who is extremely beautiful according to African criteria (the lines are all curve, the neck is long) is in perfect dooplé, and her hands are in djaon. Around her waist is the bile, a dancing object.

Izie statue, Nigeria. Height: 83cm. Georges-Jacques Haefeli Collection.

SECONDARY FORMS

Several forms, created from gestures of the arms, legs, the torso have specific and didactic forms. These are principally:

Gba
Gba Kla and Gba Zan
Gbaou
Gbou a Gbaou
Ploa Bgaou
Ziaplo a Gbaou
Naou

Gba

To an African the gba, or fork, describes the part where the tree divides into many branches, and more particularly the fork with two branches, with an angle of 180 degrees.

The gba (whose name varies according to each ethnic group) is of enormous importance in daily life. It was one of the primary utensils for gathering as in agriculture and it was also one of the essential implements in the hut or in the early rectangular dwellings.

For gathering, one of the prongs of the gba is sufficiently long to serve as a kind of handle. It can be extended with a longer shaft. The angle formed by the two prongs is between 30 to 90 degrees.

With this forked rod, the man of the forest could pick the fruits by wedging them at the angle of the gba and pulling them. He could also, as on the coffee and cocoa plantations, pull the branch downwards with the aid of the gba and pick the fruits. He could also use the gba to shake the branches and make the ripe fruit fall, as happened on the cocoa plantations.

The gba is indispensable to the farmer for clearing the fields but it has also contributed to more sedentary habits among the forest people. Before gathering the coffee and cocoa in the fields, the farmer would beat down the undergrowth with the gba before cutting it to the ground with a machete. This technique is still employed today in modern Africa, especially for preparing land to be cultivated with rice, maize and cassava.

In architecture, the gba holds up the ceiling and the other parts which fix the roof. It is a tree trunk of two to three centimetres rounded off by a fork with two equal prongs fifteen centimetres long.

African tradition divides the body in several gba:

Each limb, upper and lower, consists of seven gba:

The hand and the foot are each divided into four gba determined by the fingers and the toes.

The fifth gba is formed by the hand and the forearm at the wrist. On the lower limb it is formed at the ankle by the foot and the leg.

The sixth gba is formed at the elbow and knee respectively by the arm and forearm, the leg and the thigh.

The torso and the arm at the junction of the shoulder and the torso form the seventh upper gba; the thigh and the torso at the junction of the thigh and pelvis form the seventh lower gba.

In African dance, a movement, gesture or attitude is in gba when it displays (or ends in) a two-prong fork with a 180 degree angle.

Gba is also the symbol of struggle because there must be at least two to fight.

The drum which announces, precedes and accompanies the struggle is called the gba-goule.[4]

Gba Kla

A dancer is in gba kla (grand fork) when, with the help of his hands, he stands on his head, his legs separated in the air, forming a 180 degree angle.

Gba Zan

A dancer is in gba zan (medium fork) when:

— he is lying on the back or the stomach, his legs stretched out, wide apart, on the ground.

— lying on his back, his legs, wide apart, are raised vertically.

— lying on his back, he raises his torso and his legs supporting himself by the nape of his neck and by his hands;

— lying on his stomach, the thighs close together on the ground, the legs, wide apart, are raised vertically.

The angle formed should never exceed 180 degrees.

Gbou a Gbaou

The word gbou means hut or house and gbaou means column or trunk of the gba, a wooden or bamboo shaft of a bow or arrow.

A dancer stands in gbou a gbaou when his legs are in dooplé, the torso is erect, the head is thrown backwards, the face is djaon, his arms are raised in parallel towards the sky, the palms in djaon, almost as if he wanted to hold up the sky and stop it falling (or collapsing on the house).

Plo a Gbaou

The term describes the wooden or bamboo part of a bow. It is used in dance to describe a position which recalls a bow.

---

4   The tuning pegs which fix the skin on the barrel of the drum are also called gba because they determine the fork with the circumference of the drum. The gba is an ingenious invention in African traditional music because it enables both the skin to be fixed and the instrument to be tuned.

Ziaploa Gbaou

This name describes the wooden shaft which makes a musical bow (ziaplo).

When an African dancer has just made a bridge, he is in ziaploa gbaou. His head is thrown back gracefully, his gaze looks back, fixing the horizon at ground level. The arms are almost parallel and slightly bent giving the impression of creepers. The palms of the hand and the soles of the feet are in coula on the ground; the legs are parallel in dooplé.

The torso of the dancer is supple and lively and forms an imaginary line similar to a rainbow.

Much prized by dancers from Mali, Malinke, Guinea, Senegal and Burkina, the ziaploa gbaou is the speciality of the Sangnounou (jugglers) of western Ivory Coast.

The suppleness of the vertebral column is fundamental to the ziaploa gbaou and helps the dancer to accomplish very complex movements either in the air or on the ground.

Through an association of ideas all the movements of the vertebral column[5] are called ziaploa gbaou, recalling the bridge or bow (the back should be the interior of the bow).

Naou

Naou can mean feather (nai) but also wings, the symbol of liberty.

A Masque de Sagesse advances with slow steps. It has an extraordinary head-dress consisting of feathers and other accessories and wears over the tunic about thirty raffia skirts, three metres in size. The feathers do not signify that he is trying to escape gravity.

The meaning of the feathers is defined by the bird to which they belong.[6] They have many different meanings, from that of pure decoration to the attempt to make something fly in the air for a moment (the feathers of the arrows of the hunters). There is also the crest (dourou naou) or the flamboyant top of the human head symbolising the internal breath of cosmic and divine origin which animates thinking beings. This crest on the head-dress indicates the centre of supreme human consciousness.

The naou forms are specific to the upper limbs.

An arm is in naou when it is detached from the trunk and extended obliquely, horizontally, vertically, on the side or behind.

The arms in naou can be parallel or more wide apart. If they are rejoined at the wrists or the hands, they are no longer in naou.

---

5 The vertebral column forms a real musical bow; musical notes can be drawn from each of the vertebrae.
6 African tradition classes birds in two categories: noble birds or others. The male and female eagle are a unit, like the sparrowhawk, and belong to the first category.

Gestures in the dance

Every part of the body has a role to play in traditional African dance; the arms and the hands also have a language which complements that of the legs and the body.

The gestures, specific to the manners and customs of the continent, express the conditions of the soul and each has its own meaning which is known to the African dancers and spectators.

The richness of these gestures explains why the sign-language of the faces are non-existent and superfluous in the genuine traditional African dance.

The impassivity of the face owing to the richness of the gesture is also found in the mudras of Hindu dances.[7]

There are certain gestures which help to achieve a better interpretation of certain dances:

When during a dance step the two arms turn together from front to back in a circle, they express anger or discontent if the movement of the arms is spirited.

By contrast the same movement of the arms if it is slow, gliding, fluid and light expresses a feeling of generosity or sadness.

The arm and the hand which shake when picking up the bile (the danced object) are the gestures of the diviner in a trance.

To dance bent in two, the two arms crossed on the plexus is a symbol of senior initiation.

There is a sign used by people capable of recognising something unique through a feeling experienced in the plexus when they think or speak to each other.[8] This feeling is as precise as a face but it is necessary that these two people should have already met at least once in order to recognise and identify this sign. The form of the sign (a line, a curve, a half-circle) comprises two poles, one positive and one negative. It expresses the inclinations of each person: stable or unstable, structured or disturbed, balanced, distressed, calm.

One of the virtues of African dance is that it develops this feeling because the solar plexus is the focal point of concentration for very African dancer.

To strike the mouth with the hand in a repetitive way is a well known gesture

---

Opposite
A Teke figure representing a dancer (legs in dooplé, feet in kouitchin) holding his hands over his stomach.

Teke statuette, Republic of Congo. Height: 17.8cm. Raoul Lehuard Collection.

---

7   The Hindus are the only people in the world who learn dance from a semi-sacred book.
     According to legend the gods confided the secret of the dance to the wise man Bharata who transmitted them to the men in the Natya Sastra, or the art of the dance. This Sanskrit manuscript which has been preserved in part over two thousand years describes all the movements and positions as well as the repertory according to the different parts of the body. Thus 4,000 figurative gestures of the hands or mudras have been counted which symbolise an actual object (a fish, a bird, a flower) or a feeling (love, hate, fear, surprise).
8   Every human being emits a specific unique sign and this sign, when experienced by someone else in the plexus, gives an exact identification, like the recognition of a face.

found in Indian war dances. In Africa this gesture precedes them, it calls the attention of the gods.

To stamp and trample while hammering the ground in place is always a demonstration of uncontainable joy.

But to cross the hands on the head while walking or running is a sign of sadness or of somebody who feels lost.

On the other hand, a person sitting with his hands crossed over his head signifies relaxation and repose.

If the person sitting holds the front of his hands, the elbows on the thighs, this is a sign that he is thinking deeply and that he is a seeking a solution to an embarrassing problem.

To entwine the arms around someone's waist is a sign of joy and reunion. In embraces between boys or between girls, the arms are placed freely around the waist.

If the embraces are between boy and girl, the boy winds his arms around the lower waist of the girl as if he wanted to lift her up, while she winds her arms above those of the boy.

To take something between the thumb and the little finger is a sacred gesture specific to the diviners.

To touch someone's thumb is a gesture of initiation which belongs to the diviners and is a blessing.

To bump against one another, front to front, is a gesture of initiation, of communion.

To place the index finger under the right eye means that you should be aware of the consequences (usually bad) of your acts.

A person displeased with you points the index finger at you, the other four fingers are closed and the inside of the wrist is turned out. This means take care, beware.

For an African to present the two hands open is a sign of great honesty, the proof of an easy conscience, generosity, hospitality, greatness of heart and spirit.[9]

At the end of a judgement, before the verdict is given, the chief of the council of wise men and judges rises and goes around the assembly, his arms extended and his hands wide open, his palms offered to the public, then he goes back solemnly to his place. Through this gesture he signifies that he is telling the truth and that he will swear to tell the truth.

The hands joined together, palm against palm, at the level of the plexus, as in Christian prayer, is a dance gesture which in Africa usually has nothing to do with prayer. The fact of joining the hands triggers a physical phenomenon in the body. In effect this gesture concentrates within the organism all the energy which it produces. The right hand has a negative polarity and the left a positive. When the two hands are joined together, a circuit is established and there is no longer any phenomenon of loss. A continuous current is established from the left to the right side which results in an increasing physical energy and a power of concentration

---

9   This same gesture in contemporary modern dance is thought to represent the physical density of the air, which can either be embraced or pushed away.

which is much superior. The gesture of joined hands, palm against palm, which is associated with the soumplé, allows the body of the African dancer to function as an accumulator and dispenser of energy. Outside dance, this gesture of conserving energy is used in different ways throughout the continent. For example, an individual who wishes to express something important has the instinctive reaction to join the hands.

Arms crossed on the chest, the palms of the hand placed on the shoulders, is the authentic African gesture to indicate prayer. This gesture recalls the position of the arms on the statues of the pharaohs in ancient Egypt.

The thumb and the index finger of the right hand come together to form a circle symbolising the eternal cycle while the other fingers bend into the palm of the hand. The little finger indicates the sky and symbolises the unique source of all things.

Toesson

In Africa toesson is a typically feminine gesture.[10] It recalls the handle of a jug or a basket and has many traditional meanings.

It is not only a practical and utilitarian gesture but also a mother's gesture of affection for her child. It is the position of the mother's arms when she props her child on her hip and she can go about her various jobs while taking it with her. In this position the child can take part in the mother's life, while watching her and touching her. The child can talk to her and take her breast without causing trouble to anybody else.

Toesson becomes a code between them when the child reaches seven years old. If the child sees his mother standing in toesson with her fists on her hips then he understands immediately that she is angry with him.

Toesson is also a code between husband and wife.

The woman standing in toesson, her fists closed on the hips and her gaze sad and distant, is worried or bothered by something.

If she is standing and holds her waist closely with the thumb and the index finger (the other fingers on the body) and the arms in toesson, her husband knows that she is tired and needs rest.

If the wife stands, arms in toesson, the palms held closely on the hips, fingers pointing towards the ground, the husband knows that she has physical pain, often back-ache due to the laborious work in the fields.

Toesson is a gesture of amazement, when the person is standing, arms in toesson, the hands touching the waist with the back of the wrists, palms open and fingers pointing downwards.

Finally, toesson is the symbol of cooking utensils and, by extension, gestures of housekeeping. It is the position of the women's arms when she returns from the fields or the river, balances a gourd or a bundle on her head.

---

10 In Africa, as in many other places, men have nothing at all to do with cooking which is the sole preserve of the women.

The language of dancing animals and dancing objects

The Japanese No dances, like ancient Greek theatre, use masks in order to express emotions and, as in traditional African dance, the accessories which they use have various conventional meanings[11] according to the context.

The peculiar quality of the dancing animal is to hold itself discreetly on the head of the dancer during the dance, without ever being inhibited by this, as if it were being supported by invisible forces.

The eagle and the cock are just some of the dancing animals but there are also thousands of bees who buzz around the enormous head-dresses of some of the Masques de Sagesse when they perform certain dance steps during the great initiation ceremonies.

A dancing object is an object which the dancer holds in his hands while he is dancing.

Every decorative object and costume accessory help to mark the rhythm or to beat time. They are as much an integral part of the dance as the dancer's movements themselves. They play a definite role and have their own meanings.

It is the hands of the dancer which confer the dancing quality on the object. An object held between the teeth, for example, is not considered to be a dancing object by the Elders.

There are a limited number of objects which can be classified as dancing objects and which are part of the rites of African traditional dance. They are manifestations of the movements of the soul whose roots go back to prehistory.

Dancing objects are necessary for the execution of certain traditional African dances which are of a sacred nature and the Elders consider it a sacrilege to perform certain gestures without their dancing objects.

Moreover, certain dances were created with dancing objects and they would lose their original meanings if they were performed without their objects.

The Bile is the oldest of the dancing objects and appeared on the rocks of Tassili. It was made from the hair on the tail of a domestic animal (horse or oxen were preferred) or of a wild animal (a panther or a lion) and was the object most widely known to non-Africans.

The Gbon (a branch, preferably palm) is the dancing object specific to those original African dances which symbolise ascension, regeneration, abundance, fertility, victory, peace and communion with God.

The gbon is the most common dancing object after the bile in every African society in view of the predominant economic role which the palm tree plays.[12]

---

11 A big open fan can signify the moon, the sun, a boat, an open door; a half-open fan can mean a great mountain, a lantern, a child; a closed fan represents a sword, an umbrella, a cane or a fishing rod.

12 The palm was the symbol of fertility in Egypt and of victory in ancient Greece and Rome but it also figures in the customs and religions of many other peoples. The Christians made it the symbol of triumph over death (the martyr's palm) perhaps because of the association of its name (phoenix) with the phoenix which is born from its ashes.

In Palestine the feast of growth is traditionally linked to the palm tree. In the fourth century the Church in Jerusalem placed this feast at the beginning of Easter Week. It was introduced in the west during the seventh century by Saint Isidore of Seville and became Palm Sunday when the palms were

Palm oil is regarded as nourishment of contentment and joy and plays an important role in daily life. It is used in the making of remedies, it is promised to children if they are good, bottles of it are offered to guests during the great investiture ceremonies, the birthday meals for twins consist of rice and palm oil and during harvest time, anyone who receives help from others has to serve the palm oil throughout the meal.

Once upon a time the offer of palm oil to a prisoner meant that he was going to be set free.

Koou

The koou is a baton, often carved and painted with scenes from everyday life and with symbolic forms.

Every gla dancer has a baton approximately 1.5 metres in length which serves as a cane, the "third foot" of the mask.

The gla koou is also a symbol. The gla of wisdom represents old age with all its spiritual benefits and physical inconveniences and thus the gla koou belongs to an Elder.

Before intoning a song, the gla shakes the koou. He leans on it when he speaks to the crowd (his language is translated by an interpreter); he rises to give the orders (the baton of command), and he uses it to perform certain beo dances (the gla koou then becomes a dancing object which is essential for some dances).

Once upon a time the gla alone had the power to stop a tribal battle; today it is an arbiter. When the traditional chief is unable to resolve a dispute between two groups, the interpreter submits the case to the gla of wisdom who, after some reflection, gives him the koou. With great discretion, the interpreter gathers the opponents or the chiefs together and places the koou between them. Through respect and obedience to the spirit, the disputes or battles stop immediately, however important they may be. The opponents then place their terms before the Council of Wise Men where the problem will be settled peacefully.

Other dancing objects

Dilé is a tissue made from the bark of a tree; Djerin is a long tapered knife; Saoba (sabre, sword); Di (spear, assegai); Da (winnowing basket or sieve), Toe (basket) are also dancing objects.

Pou, a ladle or large spoon with a long handle, often wooden, which is used to serve soup or rice.

---

blessed.

Palm produces raffia and rattan; it is called plant ivory and its wood is used for construction, its leaves also decorate villages on feast days. But it also plays a social role as a symbol of peace.

Among certain African peoples one asks a favour from someone politely or simply begs pardon by saying "I will cut a palm in your honour".

Before an elephant hunt, the hunters in order to avoid accidents entwine their rifles with palm branches after silently declaring their sincere desire for peace.

In Ouebloa there is a festival called Goo. The women open the ceremony with a dance in which the only dancing object allowed is the pou. Throughout the ritual, sustained by the percussion, the dancers shake their pou and call or cry in a tragic manner to the departed.

To the Elders and according to tradition the Goo has no meaning unless the pou is used during the dance.

Occasional dancing objects

A musical instrument can temporarily become a dancing object. For example when a musician throws himself into the centre of the dance and begins to dance with his drum in his hands but without beating it, the instrument becomes a dancing object because of the context but only during the time the musician dances. For a moment it loses its role as a musical instrument.

All these eloquent gestures and dancing objects whose meaning is clear to African villagers enable African dance to express feelings and states of mind without resorting to pantomime and mime.

This richness is unfortunately either ignored by or is unknown to most contemporary choreographers.

Fire dance, Togo, March 1970. To walk on fire is to gain control over the elements. The dancers in plo and the headbands recall circles. They hold the biles (dancing objects) in their hands and their leg coverings are adorned with decoration which also evoke circles.

When I dance in dooplé
alone in the great silence of the sacred circle
formed by dancers who come from
every horizon
the pure light of Gnonsoa god of the dance
flares in my heart
and fills every atom of my body
with its radiance.

Dance, rhythm, timbre
and percussion
dominate me with all their might.

When I look
at the very heart of the divine circle
a Dancer appears
also in dooplé
who absorbs, nourishes and irradiates
the caressing fire of Guela, the greatest light of all.
This is African dance in all its splendour.
This is African dance revealed and eternal.

When my eyes
bathed in the golden white
radiantly clear eyes of the Master of the Dance
with the sweet and communicative smile
drink at the cup of pure dance
the unique prayer of the ancient Masques
which depict the earliest African dance
materialises in space
through forms
which evoke
the magnificent statues and statuettes
with their African lines.

A.T.
Nimes
October 1988